D0365225

NO LONGER PROPERTY OF
FALVEY MEMORIAL LIBRARY

PRINCIPLES and PERSUASIONS

Books by Anthony West

D. H. LAWRENCE: A CRITICAL BIOGRAPHY

THE VINTAGE

ANOTHER KIND

HERITAGE

PRINCIPLES AND PERSUASIONS

PRINCIPLES and PERSUASIONS

The Literary Essays of Anthony West

Harcourt, Brace and Company

New York

VILLANOVA COLLEGE

LIBRARY

© 1951, 1952, 1953, 1954, 1955, 1956, 1957 by Anthony West.
All rights reserved, including the right
to reproduce this book or portions thereof in any form.
First edition.
All of the essays in this book originally appeared
in The New Yorker, some of them in somewhat different form.
Library of Congress catalog card number: 57-5539.
Printed in the United States of America.

PN
511
·W44

Contents

6/7/57 Harcourt $3.60

104219

Introduction

There is a good deal of negative criticism in these essays, but I am not at all apologetic about that. My justification is in Dr. Johnson's remark that "there have been too many honeysuckle lives of Milton." Ripping the honeysuckle off Milton is an apparently destructive activity, and the sight of Robert Graves engaged upon the task is a positively alarming one. But for all its sweetness the vine in question chokes, smothers, and obscures. The naked Milton that Graves exposed to view in his brilliant essay, reprinted in the *Common Asphodel,* may be a diminished demigod, but he is the tormented and complex individual who wrote, and the facts of his behavior throw light on the creative process, and on the working of the human mind in general. Miss Ada Nisbet expressed this point as well as it can be at the end of her less passionate and perhaps even more effective attack on the honeysuckle which has been encouraged to hide Charles Dickens' fascinating psyche. In the last chapter of her scholarly study of the relationship between Dickens and his mistress, Ellen Ternan, she says that "to study the reasons for the greater maturity and depth of Dickens' later novels is to come closer to an understanding not of Dickens alone, but of the mysterious and delicate balance between strength and weakness, good and bad, light and darkness, in life itself."

Sometimes, of course, when the honeysuckle has been

cleared away a fake heroic statue made of plaster of Paris, or a ramshackle affair of old boards and stolen clothing, comes into view. This might suggest that there was little point in clearing away the honeysuckle in the first place, and that the critic has been wasting his time and his readers' time on humbug. The thing is to all appearances no more than a harmless old idol, it has given pleasure and comfort to many people in the past, and may give more in the future, why not let it alone? The reason carries one on to another appeal to Johnson, this time to his conception that the main function of literature is to teach a knowledge of life. If it is to do that it must be contributed to by writers of integrity concerned to give a truthful interpretation of their experience. There is a great deal of the truth, though something less than all of it, in Leslie Stephen's remark that "the foundation of all excellence, artistic or moral, is a vivid perception of realities and a masculine grasp of facts." The extent to which a writer will evade the realities of his relationships, and fudge and dodge facts in presenting himself to the world, gives one a good measure of his integrity. The falsifications he indulges in while fabricating the persona he presents for public consumption generally show up in his books as falsities, and if one is aware of the deliberate or compulsive distortions that shape his life one is the better equipped to judge by how much his work is a contribution to knowledge, and by how much it is a simple reflection of his psychological necessities. Biographical criticism is often destructive of a pose, and of values fabricated to sustain it, but it is, in my view, a soundly creative technique when it comes to literary assessments. It is to me, for instance, simply grotesque to treat George Eliot's work as the disinterested product of a morally healthy personality and as a valid interpretation of the life of the time; but as a creation of the psychological necessities of an essentially second-rate mind driven by ruthless egotism it is of the greatest interest. To bring that out, the life has to be related to the work. The gain of this process, though it is totally destructive to George Eliot's pretensions to be a creative artist, or even a serious thinker, is the revelation of a character almost infinitely more interesting than any product of her rather sluggish imagination. The plaster of Paris image, George Eliot taken at her own valuation, is worthless, and reverent treatment of it is a truly negative business. If we accept it as the portrait of a human being we add to our illusions about life, not to our knowledge of it.

There is a further justification for destructive criticism that Dr. Johnson could never have dreamed of; the idea of a society in which educated men were relatively unimportant could hardly have entered his mind, nor could he have imagined that literature would ever become a branch of the entertainment industry. Burckhardt could imagine both situations, and, having imagined them, baldly said that the new leisured public created by industrialism would be culture's worst enemy. It would pretend to have an appetite for literature but it would want comfort and amusement. A publishing house is a simple business today, and a publisher considers that his first responsibility is not to culture as an abstract idea but to the investors who have provided him with his working capital. He publishes a great many books which have no virtues other than that they will entertain and that they will allow him to give his backers something for their money. In the light of his preoccupation he considers a great many books to be good which are simply salable, and he describes them to the public in terms of the values of literature. The language of commerce is devitalizing and devaluing the language of criticism in an alarming way. It seems to me that one of a modern critics duties is to keep the sharp edge on words, and to maintain standards by occasionally exposing the commercial products that pass for contributions to our cultural inheritance to the full weight of aesthetic and ideological criticism. The mind bloats and softens on a diet of pap, and there is good reason for reminding the general reader from time to time that pap is pap and not good red meat. The fact that many people enjoy pap, its softness, its blandness, and its digestibility, and that some people put a great deal of sincerity and intensity into making the best pap they can is beside the point—it is a weakening and debilitating form of food. This accounts for my occasional blasts at targets of opportunity that academic criticism would pass by as beneath its notice. But then I am not writing from the haven of a learned institution for a learned audience, I am writing for a popular weekly magazine about current books as they appear, and I am addressing the general reader. With that much said I am content to let these essays speak for themselves and to let the reader judge for himself what my values are.

ANTHONY WEST

PRINCIPLES and
PERSUASIONS

Charles Evans Hughes

Charles Evans Hughes is written, to tell the truth, with a noticeable lack of literary grace, but Mr. Merlo J. Pusey has made his biography of a genuinely great man an unusually interesting book. Hughes exists for most people as an ultra-conservative corporation lawyer with altogether too great a respect for the rights of the rich and powerful, and as an unbending, humorless, and somewhat repellent personality. It is easy to understand how this misunderstanding came about. His childhood was spent in a sequence of Baptist parsonages in such towns as Oswego and Newark; their atmosphere was bleak and narrow, and poverty was an integral part of it. Hughes' father, an immigrant from Wales, whose death was to some extent due to overexcitement brought on by his efforts to get the New York police to ban Gertrude Hoffman's Salome dance at Hammerstein's, had taught his son to call him "sir" by the time he was five. Children's books had been discouraged by then, too, and the young Hughes was finding what fun he could in such light reading as Chambers' *Miscellany*. When he was approaching eight, it was still his greatest pleasure to climb up into the attic and set out on dream travels in a box drawn by a hobbyhorse with old trunk straps for reins, but even this game had to have an improving flavor, and the hobbyhorse was compelled to take him to such edifying places as were mentioned in the Bible or in approved travel books.

And on his eighth birthday his father gave him a Greek Testament with lexicon. This parental pressure was kept up even after he was in college; letters from home pursued him, warning him against worldly associations, against almost everything:

How thankful we are for God's loving care over you & how pleased that you are attentive to your studies and doing well. *Be thorough*. BE THOROUGH. BE THOROUGH. . . . In respect of your washing your neck, etc., don't ignore your feet. If you persist in washing them every day, you will cure them of sweating. . . . Don't play croquet in the evening. I was astonished that you have taken again to the "worn out game." *Well, don't play it at night. Take good care of your health in all respects*. HEED THIS WARNING!

He was taught to have a deep mistrust of the natural, instinctive side of his personality. When he was eighteen, and at Brown, and made the discovery, through some agreeable small triumphs, that he was a born orator, he wrote home about it as if the Devil had discovered a new sin for him. He assured his father that, thanks to divine mercy, he got no pleasure from the applause he earned by speaking. As his graduation approached, though, he grew more and more unwilling to become a minister, as his parents wished, and he began to prepare his escape. In doing so he delivered himself of a psychologically revealing remark: "Whatever I may do or become, there is no danger that I will ever be able to rid myself of the truths implanted in early childhood."

The Nonconformist rigidity, the excessive scrupulousness, the sense of being a righteous man in a world of sin were deeply implanted. The attitude of the elect is not one that wins friends, and it frequently created misunderstandings. When the movement to draft Hughes as the Republican candidate for President in 1916 was reaching its height, he was approached by Chief Justice White of the Supreme Court, who spoke of his wish to retire and of Wilson's intention to elevate Hughes from Associate Justice to Chief Justice in his place. This smelled of a deal, of sin, and when Hughes was drafted by the Republicans, his letter to Wilson was a rebuke to iniquity:

To the President,
   I hereby resign the office of Associate Justice of the Supreme Court of the United States.
           I am, sir, respectfully yours,
                              Charles Evans Hughes

A word of regret, a phrase indicating good will, the least intimation of human feeling, could have done no harm, but Hughes let the document stand in all its appalling coldness. He did not care what impression it made; he knew what was right. A similar incident occurred when he returned, as a lawyer in private practice, to argue a case before the Supreme Court in 1929. On the adjournment of the first session he attended, he was greeted with warmth by Chief Justice Taft, who had known, liked, and admired him for twenty years, and who, when President, had appointed him to his first term, as Associate Justice. "Hughes, my boy, I'm delighted to see you." Hughes coldly shook hands and said, "Mr. Chief Justice, I am honored to see you." Visibly hurt, Taft retired to the robing room; his mind may have gone back to the time in 1910 when he gave weeks of "prayerful consideration" (over a series of outstandingly ill-played games of golf with Henry Clay Frick) to the appointment of a Chief Justice. Hughes was the obvious man, and Taft almost appointed him, but Hughes was only forty-eight, and if he were appointed, Taft's lifelong ambition to hold the office was unlikely to be fulfilled. White, who was sixty-five, became Chief Justice. Thinking it over in the robing room, Taft must have felt that he was dealing with a man who could nurse a grudge for nineteen years, and the witnesses to the encounter must also have thought something of the kind. One of the bolder of them asked Hughes for an explanation, and got it—an answer straight from the Baptist parsonages of his youth: "I did it intentionally, as I intend to win my cases on their merits and not through friendship with the judges." The warmhearted, friendly, funny man, known and loved by his intimates, was hard to detect behind a façade made up of a mosaic of such incidents.

Hughes' physical presence had something to do with it, too. His stiff carriage and his noble beard suggested a deliberate effort to conform to nineteenth-century visual conceptions of what a great man should be, and lent him a forbidding and archaic dignity. What lay buried beneath the presence was a skinny young man, weighing only a hundred and twenty-four pounds, whose lower jaw was narrow in proportion to the rest of his face and who, in his twenties, was appearing before massive and ill-tempered judges of the old school to argue cases of great complexity against men with thirty or more years of experience. Hughes told Mr. Pusey that the beard would never have appeared had there been safety razors in the 'eighties, but when the new razors came in, the beard remained. It made its first entrance not long after an unpleasant courtroom scene in which Mr. Justice Van Brunt had attempted to browbeat Hughes for coming into court with an improp-

erly prepared case, and soon after he had become the main-
stay of his law firm. It was the defensive beard of a man
not altogether sure of himself when it took possession of
Hughes, and it was a habit, rather than the claim to the
status of a demigod that it later seemed, when, whitened
by time, it presided over the most impressive law court in
the world.

Hughes' reputation as an ultra-conservative corporation
lawyer is harder to explain. The charge that he was too
good a friend of big business was first made by William
Randolph Hearst's papers when Hughes was chosen to in-
vestigate the New York gas and electric-light companies.
He had not figured in public life before and little was
known about him, except that he had experience of commercial law and that he went to the Baptist church that
Rockefeller attended. Hearst added two and two to make
nine, and attacked the choice. Hughes exposed the utilities
so effectively, and with such obvious benefit to the people
of New York, that he was next asked to undertake an
investigation into the scandalous practices of the New
York insurance companies. Hughes showed that they were
swindling the policyholders, wasting their money in extravagant overhead, gambling recklessly with their assets,
financing the campaigns of well-disposed politicians, and
bribing legislators. Among others who suffered damage
from his inquiries was Thomas Fortune Ryan. Ryan had
persuaded the naïve and foppish James Hazen Hyde to sell
him five hundred and two shares in Equitable Life for two
and a half million dollars. Hughes made it plain that since,
by law, these shares could earn only thirty-five hundred
dollars a year, what Ryan was paying for was control of
the company's assets, which he hoped to involve in his

speculations. Hughes followed up this inquiry by rewriting the state's insurance laws. New York policyholders thus became the best protected in the world, and maneuvers such as Ryan had planned became impossible. Hughes attracted so much attention by his handling of the investigation and by his obvious devotion to the public interest that he was drafted as the Republican candidate for governor in the 1906 election, to run against Hearst. Hearst campaigned as the friend of the people; Hughes, according to his papers, was a tool of the trusts and had been bribed by Ryan to run the insurance investigation in his interest. Hughes' shoestring campaign cost him six hundred and nineteen dollars; Hearst spent five hundred thousand dollars, and lost. From then on, whenever Hughes came into the news, the charge that he was a friend of big business was repeated wherever a Hearst paper was printed.

As governor, Hughes established a record of liberal legislation equalled only by the elder La Follette in Wisconsin. He put through pioneer measures bringing about effective state control of utilities; he pioneered the planning of public hydroelectric-power projects; he brought in the first workmen's-compensation bills to become law in the United States; he introduced shorter-hours bills, bills further regulating child labor, and in all signed fifty-six model labor laws during his two terms. This progressive achievement was buried in the statute books, and if lawyers understood what he had done, few members of the public did.

Hughes left Albany to go on to the splendid obscurity of the Supreme Court as an Associate Justice, and his achievements there were again obvious to only a limited public; few people who do not have to do so read the Court's majority and dissenting opinions. Hughes inadvertently, as

Mr. Justice Brandeis pointed out, did big business a good turn in one case, because he was under the impression that price cutting was a weapon that small stores could use to defend themselves against chains. But this is a single case. In the Alabama peonage case, the Arizona anti-alien labor-statute case, the Oklahoma Jim Crow-car case, and the De Jonge v. Oregon free-assembly case, he showed himself to be an advanced liberal. He consistently refused to interpret the freedom-of-contract clause in the Fourteenth Amendment as business wanted it interpreted—to burke the healthy growth of the trade unions and to prevent the regulation of hours and wages by the states. His line of thought is most clearly shown, though, in the hundred-page majority opinion he wrote in the Minnesota rate cases and the majority opinion he wrote in the Shreveport case. They are without color and drama, being complex definitions of the powers of the Interstate Commerce Commission to regulate railway tariffs, but they are, nonetheless, vital episodes in a social revolution. They are also an important passage in the sequence of opinions that introduced a new dimension, that of the dominant public interest, into the law, and in giving a final legal authority to the social concepts behind the I.C.C. they expanded the Constitution so that the federal government was enabled to take control of national economic policy. They opened the way for Wilson's new agencies—the Federal Reserve System, the Federal Trade Commission—and for the Clayton Antitrust Act, and they are an essential part of the legal platform on which the New Deal was erected.

Had Hughes remained with the Court, he would without doubt now be known as a great liberal constitutional lawyer, but he resigned when he was drafted by the Republicans

for President, and after his defeat he vanished into that
limbo into which failed Presidential candidates, like fired
generals, usually fade gently away. When he emerged from
it, as Secretary of State in Harding's Cabinet, in 1921, he
was in strange company for a progressive. He was not one
of the group—including the questionable Harry Daugherty,
the inadequate and possibly honest Edwin Denby, and the
interminably garrulous and fatally dishonest Albert Fall—
that called the President Wernie. He belonged to the group
whose members Harding always addressed as Mister—
Mister Hughes, Mister Mellon, Mister Hoover. Yet even
association with that superior band did him little good in
the long run, and gave color for the first time to the suspicion that he was at heart a conservative. His policy while
he was Secretary of State supported the suspicion. Apart
from his brilliant negotiation of the naval-disarmament
treaty, and a phase of support for the League of Nations,
he gave little evidence of being aware of the new pattern
of international relationships that was developing. In the
end, he went along with the prevailing isolationism, and
resisted all but a minimal coöperation with the ailing League.
And when he resigned from office in 1925 and went back
into private practice, he at last gave basis to the charges
Hearst had so often made. For the next four years he was
a corporation lawyer.

When, in 1930, Hoover reappointed him to the Supreme
Court as Chief Justice, it was that brief interlude and his
service in Harding's Cabinet, rather than the substance of
his career, that were remembered. There were violent pro-
tests, led by Senators Blease, Borah, and Norris, that the
appointment was another in a series of reactionary moves
to pack the Court with defenders of the constitutional rights

of property and private interest. It is true that the Court then contained a formidable bloc of constitutional literalists, composed of Sutherland, Van Devanter, McReynolds, and Butler, but Hughes did not join it. He sided rather with the group whose legal philosophy he shared, which included Brandeis, Stone, Holmes, and (after Holmes' retirement) Cardozo. He believed, like Marshall, that the Constitution was "intended to endure for ages to come, and, consequently, to be adapted to the various crises of human affairs." In spite of this, Hughes later seemed, from the outside, to be leading a reactionary Court into battle against the New Deal on the side of literalism in the cases that torpedoed the N.R.A., the Agricultural Adjustment Administration, and the first Frazier-Lemke farm-mortgage act. But it has to be remembered that the whole apparatus of the New Deal, which changed a free economy under the limited control of the states into a controlled economy under the federal thumb, was improvised in three months by a handful of fantastically overworked men. It was, naturally, rich in error. In the hot-oil case, the federal government was attempting to defend the punitive actions it had taken in accordance with a section of the Petroleum Code that had been omitted by a clerical error from the final draft. The N.R.A. case involved an attempt to use the federal powers over interstate commerce to punish a Brooklyn poultry house that had killed a sick chicken and sold it to a dealer in Brooklyn. And the A.A.A. rested on an impossible interpretation of Congressional power to tax as the justification for a sweeping program to regulate farm production. It was not a matter of conflict between progressive and reactionary opinion, as Roosevelt felt when he proposed to pack the Court, but a recognition of legislative errors that could not be reconciled with the Constitution in any way. Though it is this early collision with the New Deal, and Hughes' masterly campaign to defeat Roosevelt's subsequent attempt to make the Court an instrument of the Executive, that are the most memorable incidents of his leadership of the Court, his real achievement is buried in the less spectacular opinions supporting the New Deal, which stretched reasonable interpretation of the Constitution to the utmost to permit the expansion of federal and state powers to meet the problems of the economic crisis and to fit the new necessities of industrial society. The story of the growth of Hughes' mind from the time he escaped his father's domination until, under the influence of Holmes, he became the collaborator of Brandeis and Cardozo in a great period of creative lawmaking is the story of the growth of the law and an illumination of the effective role of liberalism in modern history.

Winston Churchill

In his preface to *Triumph and Tragedy*, Winston Churchill explains that he has given the sixth and concluding volume of his *The Second World War* this title because the overwhelming victory of the Grand Alliance failed to bring a general peace. There is as good reason to give it the same title if it is considered not as history but as the final volume of a unique political autobiography. The first section of this political biography was written as long ago as 1923, as Volume I of *The World Crisis*, a history of the First World War, and it was immediately recognized for what it was by Mr. Arthur Balfour, the delicate thinker and incompetent politician who was then one of the leaders of the Conservative Party. He was, he wrote, "immersed in Winston's brilliant autobiography, disguised as a history of the universe." There was malice behind the remark, for Mr. Churchill was the symbol of the greatest blunder Mr. Balfour had until then made in his political career. But it was a relaxed malice, since Mr. Balfour had already taken a more than adequate revenge, which had so affected Mr. Churchill's career that anyone would have been justified in thinking that it had been brought to an end. It is hard to realize now that the first volume of *The World Crisis* was written in political limbo by a man who seemed to have no political future at all.

Mr. Churchill had entered into the war with resounding

13

brilliance as First Lord of the Admiralty. It was due to his foresight and organizing power that the Navy was, unlike the other services, ready and mobilized when, on August 4, 1914, England declared war on Germany. His future as a leader of the Liberal Party and as Prime Minister seemed certain. The most intelligent of his colleagues in the Liberal Cabinet was sure that he would leave Lloyd George far behind. He ended the war a nonentity, at the head of the Ministry of Munitions, altogether overshadowed by his Welsh rival, and in the 1922 elections he suffered temporary extinction. Standing for Parliament in Dundee, he ran more than ten thousand votes behind a prohibitionist, notable only for the extreme narrowness of his mind, who, when he had first challenged Mr. Churchill, before the war, had been able to muster no more than seven hundred votes in the constituency. Defeats the next year in West Leicester and the year after that in Westminster followed, and his rejection seemed final. The irony of his situation was that he had ruined himself by the exercise of the qualities that were to make him a great leader and by his recognition of the hinge on which the destiny of the world was turning.

The pattern of his disaster is easy to trace. In the eighteen-nineties, he had launched himself on a career as a professional soldier in the old Army, then still dominated by the ideas of the catastrophic Duke of Cambridge (he was against teaching, or even allowing, infantrymen to take cover in maneuvers, on the ground that "wars are not won by jacks-in-boxes"), and when he had seen it in action, he abandoned it for the role of critic and became a journalist and a war correspondent. He was related by blood to Army families and he was pushed by petticoat influence. He owed

his presence at Omdurman under Kitchener to the wire-
pulling of Lady Jeune, a friend of his mother's. The criticisms he made in public of the conduct of the Omdurman
campaign, and later on of the Boer War, seemed to many
like treachery to his class and to his friends. At the end of
the Boer War, he had established himself in the minds of
many regular soldiers as a self-advertising boomster without any sense of loyalty or decency. Promotion in the
Army of that time was largely a matter of influence, and
the regular soldiers were closely allied to the leading Conservative families. When he took his seat as a Conservative
Member of Parliament after the war, he was already an
object of suspicion. He deepened the suspicion with extraordinary rapidity by making a series of telling attacks on
his own Party's Minister for War, the far from brilliant Mr.
St. John Brodrick, who is chiefly remembered for his attempt to saddle the British Army with a ridiculous cap of a
German type. The attacks were more than justified, but
they scarcely won Mr. Churchill the affection of his Party
chiefs. He further affronted every soldier by saying that as
things stood, England's only defense was the Navy. In
March, 1904, he got his reward. When he rose in debate
to speak against the Conservative tariff policy, Mr. Balfour,
the Party leader, and all his followers walked out of the
chamber. Soon after he had received this unmistakable
notice to quit, Mr. Churchill entered the House, crossed
the strip of empty floor that divided the seats of the two
great parties, and took his place on the Liberal benches beside Mr. Lloyd George.

It is impossible to overstress the importance of this incident in Mr. Churchill's career. Its immediate effect was
to make Mr. Balfour feel about him as Mr. Farley came to

feel about Roosevelt, and Truman to feel about Mr. James Byrnes. This feeling became a passionate hatred when, two years later, the Conservative Party was swept out of office and the Liberal Party was swept in by the most overwhelming landslide in the history of English politics. Completely impotent, and from amid the wreckage of his Party, Mr. Balfour watched his candidate for oblivion rapidly climb the ladder to Cabinet rank. In 1910, Mr. Churchill became Home Secretary and, as a further act of treachery to his class, took a leading part in laying the foundations of the welfare state. It was clear to everybody that either he or Lloyd George would succeed Mr. Asquith as Prime Minister. At the age of thirty-six, Mr. Churchill was at the top of the tree.

But the higher he climbed, the more his energy and his appetite for life worked against him. The restlessness and comprehensiveness of his mind could not find full exercise in his own Ministry. He was naturally endowed with the gifts of a Prime Minister. He disintegrated the Cabinet machine by submitting endless lengthy memorandums on the concerns of other Ministers. Time and again, he exasperated Mr. Asquith by obstructing the procedure of Cabinet meetings with his flow of suggestions and criticisms. And his sense of urgency and his relish for being the man on the spot led him into adventures that made him seem preposterous. Clad in a fur-collared coat and a top hat, he became grotesquely involved with the police, the Fire Brigade, and a platoon of the Scots Guards in the siege of two London gunmen who had barricaded themselves in a house on Sidney Street. When his secretary asked him what he supposed he had been doing, he felt able to reply, "Don't be cross; it was such fun." But the earnest people in the country took a less happy view of the fact that he had turned out the Scots Guards to handle what was properly a police matter. They became further alarmed when, in 1911, the Home Secretary responded to the threat of a general railroad strike by ordering rapid and spectacular troop movements. The Agadir crisis was growing in intensity, and war with Germany seemed imminent. It was vital that the outbreak of war should not find the nation's railroads at a standstill, and the use of troops to keep traffic moving was completely justified. But the public did not know how great the danger was; to its mind, Mr. Churchill was boyishly introducing a new and ugly element into the English social picture. The Army itself, antagonized by the Liberal government's reforms, which were challenging the influence of the Conservative military families, was showing an increasing tendency toward political activity. The public had become thoroughly wary of quasi-military adventurers, and because of the railroad episode it included Mr. Churchill in its dislikes. Mr. Asquith hurriedly transferred Mr. Churchill from the Home Office to the Admiralty.

In the three years that were left to prepare for war, Mr. Churchill did magnificent work, and the Navy was ready when war was declared. But the cloak of security concealed this important fact from the public. Even his colleagues, who were aware of what he had done and what it meant, were amused by his obsession, after his successful mobilization of the fleet, with the whereabouts of a single German battle cruiser, the *Goeben*, which had disappeared from sight in the Mediterranean. They thought he was being boyish again, eager for a scrap and eager to get headlines for the fleet. They did not realize that the course of history depended upon the *Goeben*. It suddenly turned up off Constantinople, and the Turkish government, looking into the muzzles of its guns, ended its hesitation and went into the war on the German side. Thus the Dardanelles was closed and Russia was cut off from the Western Allies. Mr. Churchill proliferated with plans to undo this disaster. He proposed a descent on Schleswig-Holstein, with the seizure of the Kiel Canal and the opening of the Baltic route to Russia as its aim. When the difficulties of launching this blow, so near the centers of German strength, became obvious, Mr. Churchill turned toward forcing a passage past Constantinople into the Black Sea. The reopening of the Dardanelles replaced the sinking of the *Goeben* as his obsession. The public knew nothing of all this, either, or of what was in Mr. Churchill's mind. When it next saw him, he was marching through the streets of Antwerp, wearing a fur hat with a plume and the sort of fantastically befrogged uniform affected by Hussars and lion tamers, at the head of the Naval Division. It consisted of eight thousand men, only two thousand of whom were fully trained; the rest were reservists, many of them without rifles. With this unlikely force, Mr. Churchill was to seize and hold the port of Antwerp. The public was not told for a long time afterward that he had been promised relief by an army of thirty to forty thousand men if he could hold the port for four days—relief that never arrived. To the public, he appeared involved in a foolish effort to turn the German Army aside from its drive on Paris, and they blamed him for the heavy losses the Naval Division suffered. The First Lord of the Admiralty, they felt, had no more business being in Antwerp and on the firing line than the Home Secretary had had in Sidney Street.

Mr. Arthur Balfour and the Conservatives prepared for vengeance. They took it when the attempt to open up the Dardanelles failed. Mr. Churchill had overborne the opposition of the admirals of the fleet and of the generals who wanted every available man for France. He was the only responsible figure in public life who saw the importance of the operation, and by his insistence on it he lost all support inside the Government and out. His enemies organized resistance to it, and its execution was hampered by what amounted to sabotage. By the time the attempt was called off, the fleet had suffered heavy losses and the pick of the New Zealand and Australian armies had been destroyed on the Gallipoli beaches. And nothing had been achieved. When the Conservatives attacked, Mr. Churchill was dismissed with hardly a murmur of dissent. As he went out to France to join a regiment in the line, the dark shadow of complete failure lay on him. His commanding officer greeted him coldly and, after half an hour's silence, remarked, "I think I ought to tell you that we were not at all consulted in the matter of your coming to join us."

It was a situation from which no ordinary man would have recovered, and Mr. Churchill did his level best to see that he did not recover by continuing to flout popular opinion as soon as he resumed office. Returned to Parliament in the first postwar election, in 1918, he made, as Liberal Secretary of State for War and for Air, a futile attempt to undo the failure of the Dardanelles. He had seen Russia collapse when it was cut off from Western supplies of arms and munitions, and after Germany was defeated, he tried to reverse the course of history by building up the White Russian forces that were fighting the Soviets. The war-weary and exhausted public would have none of his bracing summons to further efforts and a new war. He was assailed from all sides. Mr. Osbert Sitwell wrote bitter satirical verses against him. The trades unions saw to it that his munition ships were strikebound at their docks; the unhappy British troops in Archangel and the Caucasus began to sport red rosettes and clamored to come home; Mr. David Low cartooned Churchill as a pint-size Napoleon wearing an enormous watch chain covered with medals that spelled out the word "Defeat." The Liberal Party, disintegrated by the strains of war and by Mr. Lloyd George's increasingly eccentric leadership, was swinging toward pacifism and had no use for Mr. Churchill; the growing Labour Party, with half a century of anti-Czarist sympathies behind it, detested him as a reactionary; and Mr. Arthur Balfour was still a power among the Conservatives. Beaten at the polls in 1922, Mr. Churchill was a man without a party and again without a future.

All this is part of the background to the six volumes of which *Triumph and Tragedy* is the last. It provides the clue to the lonely struggle that makes the first volume, *The Gathering Storm*, which takes the reader back to the early nineteen-thirties, such a moving story. Mr. Churchill had, of course, by that time come home to the Conservative Party and had held a Cabinet post under Mr. Baldwin. But he was not altogether trusted. He was still paying for the day he crossed the floor of the House of Commons and took his place beside Mr. Lloyd George. When he raised his voice against the slow drift to disaster over which Mr. Baldwin and his Defense Ministers presided so complacently, the past came vividly alive. It was the same old story; here he was calling himself a Conservative and embarrassing the Party leaders. The tradition of his untrustworthiness grew. Hindsight has lent an authority to his speeches on military matters that they did not have when he made them. He spoke to the House as the adventurer of Sidney Street and Antwerp, as the man who had put the Anzacs through the mincer on the Gallipoli beaches and who had attempted to invest the peaceful General Strike of 1926 with the drama of revolution by urging that the troops be brought out again. The rhetoric of *The World Crisis* also stood between him and his audience. He was like the war horse that answered ha-ha to the trumpets; he had a taste for that kind of thing and reasonable men did not. He was listened to with amused toleration as the baby-faced Napoleon Mr. Low had constructed in the public imagination. No democracy has ever seen anything like the recovery of position and prestige by a completely discredited politician that is the theme of *The Gathering Storm*, or any triumph of personality like that revealed in the succeeding volumes, in which Mr. Churchill stands as the embodied will of the British people to fight the German war on to a victorious end. But the elements Mr. Churchill rightly calls tragic are all there, too; the past was to prove irretrievable.

The old memories recur as a minor theme in the third volume, *The Grand Alliance*. The Australian government led by Mr. Menzies fell in 1941 because it could not bring its troops back from the Middle East rapidly enough to still popular agitation. Mr. Curtin's government, which had come into office on the strength of this issue, hurried them home in spite of the fact that their withdrawal imperilled the situation in Egypt and the Middle East and threw the British plans in that theatre out of gear for several precious months. There was not the faintest possibility of leaving Australian troops under Mr. Churchill's leadership in the

Mediterranean theatre; the bitter words of the Australian official history of the First World War could not be forgotten, and the memory of the Dardanelles had done its work. The theme repeats itself with growing importance in the ensuing volumes as the American contribution to the war became paramount. The American Chiefs of Staff were never able to see Churchill as anything more than the architect of disaster at the Dardanelles, the amateur with a taste for unproductive ventures and sideshows. It was because of this belief that General Alexander's army in Italy was whittled away and Churchill's proposal to let him attempt to capture Vienna before the Russians could take it was frustrated.

As victory approached, the theme of Mr. Churchill's ancient fear of the Soviets became as important as the Dardanelles theme. He introduced it himself with minutes and memorandums harping on the necessity of having the armies of the Western Allies meet the Russians as far to the East as possible. As the scales tip toward the Allied side, his warnings assume greater force. And they fall on deaf ears. The memory of his 1919 venture against Russia cannot be effaced: The old man has always wanted a war with Russia; it is just pretty Fanny's way. The warnings, the appeals for haste on the roads to Berlin, Prague, and Vienna, sit bleakly on the pages of Mr. Churchill's last two volumes, *Closing the Ring* and *Triumph and Tragedy*. The jocular reactions of Mr. Roosevelt and the American field commanders are recorded elsewhere. It was amusing, they seemed to feel, to see how persistently the old boy tried to drag the United States into serving the aims of British imperialism.

The 1919 theme became dominant in the hour of vic-

tory, when Mr. Churchill, licensed by Stalin, who had sold
out his Athenian followers in exchange for being given a
free hand in Rumania by the Western powers, employed
the British Army to suppress a Communist revolution in
Greece. Instantly all the old memories and suspicions were
revived. The United States press and administration turned
on him, and so did the British people. Here was the man
who had used troops in the railroad strike and in the General Strike. Here was the man who would try to hold India
down with bayonets. Here was the old reactionary who
put the troops into Russia last time. We won't give him
another chance. Aneurin Bevan's speeches attacking Mr.
Churchill along these lines did more than anything else to
win Labour the election that brought an end to his term of
office as the national leader and reduced him to the role of
spectator in the decisive months of armistice, in which the
future of Europe was decided—decided on the one hand
by the Russians, who had a consistent program for securing
a major place in the center of Europe, and on the other by a
crumbling alliance primarily concerned with rapid demobi-
lization and the restoration of peacetime economies. At the
end of *Triumph and Tragedy*, the leading figure on the
European stage vanishes as abruptly as a puppet is whisked
off the stage of a Punch-and-Judy show. His past had for
the moment overtaken him again.

The final irony, which brings the story to the level of
tragedy, is that even had the election been won, victory in
the war would have confronted Mr. Churchill with the
darkest moment of his past. Though his courage and integrity had enabled him to return from the depths and win
more power and a greater trust than had ever before been
placed in the hands of an English statesman, there was no

undoing the work of destiny. He had been able to return because Germany had once again become the ruling military power in Europe, and he returned pledged to defeat the German war machine. There was no way of doing it without destroying Germany's military power, and once that was destroyed, a vacuum existed in Europe that Russia alone could fill. And because Mr. Churchill had been frustrated first in his attempt to force the Dardanelles, and then in his attempt to intervene in the Russian civil war, it was a Sovietized Russia that would fill it. His triumph was inescapably the triumph of everything he most loathed. His history of the war shows plainly his growing consciousness of this dilemma and his unfaltering courage in the face of it.

There are blots on the chronicle, moments of the petulance that has starred Mr. Churchill's whole career with savage verbal annihilations of those who have been unlucky enough to irritate him, and the unhappy record of the meaningless and aimless slighting of General de Gaulle. But these are minor blemishes, and he stands out as a magnificent figure, large enough to see the world as a whole and capable of dominating it. His language is apt to be rich and overblown, teetering at times on the edge of platform trickery, but the imagination behind the language is heroic, and it is one of the few that have so far appeared adequate to the sweep and grandeur of the new scale of world affairs.

Appeasement

Claude G. Bowers' account of the six years during which he was United States Ambassador to the Spanish republic, entitled *My Mission to Spain*, is interesting for a variety of reasons. The first is that Mr. Bowers' tour of duty ran from 1933 to 1939, so that he was in an especially favorable position to witness the whole process of the establishment, in blood and misery, of what has proved to be the most enduring of the European Fascist dictatorships. This process has been falsified in this country as industriously as the history of the 'twenties has been falsified in Russia, and it is good to have an account of it put on paper by an eyewitness who is also a historian of distinction. The widely accepted picture shows liberal weakness and ineptitude destroying a working democracy, first by flirting with Socialism and then by failing to resist Communist violence, until at last that gallant gentleman General Franco was forced to clean house and, against his will, to revolt. There is not one element of truth in this fable, as Mr. Bowers demonstrates.

The Spanish Center and Right Wing parties had discredited themselves by one squalid and grotesque scandal after another since they had come into power, in 1933, and they had lost the elections held in February of 1936 to a coalition rather less to the left of Center than Roosevelt's first administration, a coalition that thereupon set up a government that included no Communists and not even an evolutionary Socialist of the Norman Thomas variety. It was, in fact, a liberal administration with a mildly progressive flavor. Long before it took office, General José Sanjurjo, military leader of the Fascist movement before Franco took over, and Juan March, the wealthy Spanish Rightist, had been in contact with the Nazis in Germany and the Fascists in Italy, to arrange for united action if the Right Wing should lose the elections. This was not to be a counter-attack against a triumphant Communist regime; it was to be a Fascist assault upon a constitutionally elected democracy. Between the elections of 1936 and the summer of 1936, while the Fascists were completing their plans for their uprising, there was a swing away from extremism inside the Spanish Left Wing parties, and in June the moderationist Indalecio Prieto won a resounding victory over the extremist Largo Caballero in the Socialist Party elections and took over the control of the Party, by then the major political organization in Spain, from him. The Fascists, however, had no intention of letting the republic pursue even a course of moderation, and their strong-arm gangs of *pistoleros*, organized by the Monarchist Calvo Sotelo, arranged outrages and assassinations of Left Wing leaders almost every day. These provocations produced the retaliations they were designed to bring about, and the Fascists could thus pretend that the Left was bringing Spain to anarchy.

The revolt was the result of one of these sequences of provocation and retaliation. In July of 1936 a lieutenant of the government's Assault Guards was shot down by a band of Fascist gunmen in broad daylight as he stood with his arm round his wife at his front door, and at four the next morning Calvo Sotelo, himself the cause of so much killing, was taken from his house and shot by a group of Assault Guards. The Franco revolt followed. Nine days later, the first German planes were on their way to Spain, and Hitler's drive to establish the Belsen-Dachau culture throughout Europe had begun. Within three months the Nazi Condor Legion had been installed in Spanish bases. The fabricators of the Spanish myth, who pretend that General Franco was the leader of a crusade to rescue Christian Spain from the horrors of Communist atheism, choose to forget the violence and persistence with which his principal allies conducted their own struggle with the church, and their complete disregard of Christian values. Even if Communists and other Left Wing extremists, such as the Anarchists and Syndicalists, did rally to the Republican side when the civil war broke out, their atheism is neatly balanced in the account. The Reds who came in on the Republican side may have turned to Russia for the source of their anti-religious sentiments, but Franco's Falangists took them direct from Hitler, whose words are unmistakable:

In Madrid the sickening odor of the heretic's pyre remained for more than two centuries mingled with the air one breathed. If a revolution breaks out again in Spain, one must see in it the natural reaction to an interminable series of atrocities. One cannot succeed in conceiving how much cruelty, ignominy, and falsehood the intrusion of Christianity has spelt for this world of ours.

If the misdeeds of Christianity were less serious in Italy, that's because the people of Rome, having seen them at work, always knew exactly the worth of the Popes before whom Christendom prostrated itself. For centuries no Pope died except by the dagger, poison, or the pox.

Extremism, whatever its color, speaks in the end one language and proceeds inexorably to the betrayal of the human spirit. In his portraits of the leaders of the republic Franco destroyed, Mr. Bowers shows that many of them were devout Christians, for whom such opinions and such utterances were unthinkable—moderate and reasonable men who wished for nothing but a peaceful healing of their country's tragic divisions.

Mr. Bowers is not dispassionate or impartial in his account of the long-drawn-out war that followed this Fascist rising; he was wholeheartedly on the side of the liberals, and he considers their abandonment by the democracies an appalling error. The people of Spain rose to the support of their government, and for three years they fought against the imported Italian and German armies and the Moorish troops Franco brought in from Spanish North Africa. Mr. Bowers believes that if at any time during that three years the Loyalists had been allowed to buy arms in quantity they would have won their fight, and that it was because Britain, France, and the United States denied them arms that they were beaten in the end. He came to this conclusion at the start, when the military *coup d'état* seemed to have failed and the Spanish people showed where their sympathies lay, and he told the State Department what he thought. He went on telling the State Department what he thought for the whole three years, without result. He saw his liberal Spanish friends slowly wakening to the realization that they were being sold down the river, and that the Western democracies intended only to prevent all aid from reaching them while the republic for which they had such great hopes was murdered by the Fascist rebels. Neither

England, nor France, nor the United States would help out
a democracy that was fighting for its life. It is one of the
more disgusting episodes of modern history, and it is hard
to read about it without sharing Mr. Bowers' anger and
distress.

But it has to be admitted that anger and history do not go
well together; the emotion, natural though it is, obscures
the issues and introduces certain oversimplifications. Mr.
Bowers enlarges on the perfidy of France and England
in the betrayal of the Spanish republic and is somewhat
reserved about the American role. The French and British
maneuvers that deprived the republic of desperately needed
aircraft and arms are particularized with loving distaste, but
the American parallels are omitted. There is no mention of
the State Department's refusal to issue an export license for
forty war planes ordered by Greece, though intended for
the Spanish government. After this deal was frustrated,
the Spanish government tried another tactic; it ordered
some Canadian aircraft through the Turkish government.
These planes were to be powered with American engines,
and again the State Department intervened; export licenses
for the engines were refused, and the deal collapsed. In
1938, when Franco was driving on Catalonia, the Russians
made an attempt to secure two million dollars' worth of
aircraft and engines for the Republicans from the United
States; the export licenses were again refused by the State
Department when the Russians declined to give a guarantee
that the shipment was not intended for Loyalist Spain.

One can see why Mr. Bowers would like to forget these
incidents, but it is harder to see why he should omit some
others. In 1937, Italian submarines masquerading as rebel
vessels sank a number of ships in the Mediterranean, and

the British and French took action that Mr. Bowers describes in this way:

Hastily, a conference of all the Mediterranean powers was called, and while Italy would not attend without Germany, which was not invited because not a Mediterranean country, the other nations sat down at Nyon and agreed to drastic action. War vessels were to patrol the sea and sink any submarine attacking any ship not Spanish, or any that refused to show its colors. This served for a while. But the bombing of ships continued until a British ship was sent to the bottom with its crew.

This does not make it quite clear that British and French destroyers depth-charged a number of submarines and sank at least one in implementing the Nyon agreement. The positive action is glossed over, and this is not the only case in which it is pushed into the background to strengthen the picture of French and British pusillanimity. It is a universal tendency to be kinder to oneself than to one's friends, and Mr. Bowers affords some pleasing examples of the contrast between common prudence and the spirit of appeasement. He was aboard the United States warship *Cayuga*, which was evacuating American civilians from the town of Gijón, when a ship appeared on the horizon. Field glasses were pressed into service and the vessel was identified.

"It's the Cervera [a rebel warship], probably returning to shell the town again," they reported. It was approaching at considerable speed. Since, in the absence of a consul at Gijón to assemble our nationals, we would have to search the town with deliberation, it was manifest that nothing could be thoroughly done under the guns of the rebel ship. Besides, with the Cayuga in the line of fire, we might easily be involved in an incident, or our appearance at the moment of the reappearance of the

Cervera might be misunderstood. We decided to go on to Vigo and stop at Gijón on the way back.

The calculations are understandable; they are, indeed, precisely those the execrated Mr. Chamberlain was then making on a greater scale. The incident from which he and Bonnet shrank was rather larger—the war that was to consume the wealth and power of France, to deprive England of half its wealth and all its Asiatic empire, to establish Bolshevik Russia as the dominant power in Europe and Asia, and to bring about the deaths of millions of men and women. Mr. Chamberlain, seeing this future implacably bearing down on him, may perhaps be forgiven for having, so to speak, wanted "to go on to Vigo and stop at Gijón on the way back." The question of who is in a position to rebuke him is a delicate one, and though Mr. Bowers does not hesitate, it is possible to feel uneasy about the moral basis of his criticism. A few months after the collapse of the Spanish republic, Mr. Chamberlain admitted the futility of his policies and declared war on Germany. The United States government did not, and it made no move until Poland, Belgium, Holland, France, Denmark, and Norway had been conquered and occupied by Nazi and Fascist armies. Mr. Bowers did not resign from the service in protest during these two bitter years, he did not resign in protest against his country's indifference to the fate of Spain and Czechoslovakia. All things considered, it is strange to find that a man who must have been acquainted with the spirit of '39 and '40 should find the spirit of Munich hard to understand. It was a spirit of indecision and weakness from which no country was exempt, and which every free country that had experienced the point-less loss and destruction of modern war was bound to share. The index of the extent to which the spirit permeated a country was the severity of its loss in the First World War, and its origin is perhaps not in the realm of morality at all.

Functional History

T. Harry Williams' *Lincoln and His Generals* is a curious and occasionally amusing book that sets out to examine Lincoln's merits as a war leader but that is perhaps more successful as a summary of the intracommand feuds and intrigues into which his generals plunged with such enthusiasm. The historical basis of the book is as odd as the human behavior it describes, since it is an attempt to evaluate Lincoln from what the author calls "the perspective" of modern war. It seems axiomatic that the conduct of a historical figure can be judged only in relation to the conditions of his time. What makes nonsense of Shaw's Julius Caesar is that he is no Roman but a late-nineteenth-century liberal overflowing with concepts that he could not have derived from anything but a wide reading of post-Renaissance humanitarian and rationalist literature. He could not have had the ideas about power and the use of it that Shaw puts into his mouth unless he had read the posthumous accounts of his own life by Suetonius and Plutarch and had compared them with the best biographies of such persons as Cromwell, Frederick the Great, and Napoleon.

Shaw's Caesar is a dictator judged, to borrow Mr. Williams' phrase and twist it a little, from the perspective of a modern political problem of leadership. Because the problem was not Caesar's but that of the educated minority political party to which Shaw belonged, the play creates a

33

brand-new character; successful though it is on its own
level as a *coup de théâtre*, it has nothing to do with history. Lincoln is so much closer to us in time that it seems
legitimate to think of him as a modern politician and to
judge him in terms of existing political and state mecha-
nisms. But his main problems as a leader of the first modern war are as historically remote from those that confront
a modern war leader as are Julius Caesar's. Lincoln's war
machine was improvised from what amounted to scratch
in almost exactly the same way that Caesar raised his forces
for his war against Pompey the Great. The governmental
use of statistics, which is the basis of modern war leadership, had barely begun. Had Lincoln been using today's
practices and techniques, he would have had the key to the
war on his desk in the form of a memorandum about manpower just as soon as it was clear what states were aligned
against him. It would have told him that the Confederacy
had a million males of the right age for military service and
that the corresponding group he could draw on numbered
four million. Another memorandum would have summarized for him the technical resources of the opposed powers,
and within the hour he and his Cabinet would have been
able to discuss with the Chiefs of Staff the military situation and to make plans for organizing the superiority of
men and material to crush the South. If Lincoln had been
presented with statistical and geopolitical analyses of the
situation at the beginning of the war, it is likely that a
clear-cut plan for its conduct would have appeared at once.
It is almost impossible now to see any better solution to the
strategic problem than the one, hallowed by success, into
which he and the Union command drifted in the course of
the war. The solution was certainly not arrived at by the

thinking processes of such a war leader as Churchill or the composite brain power of a modern General Staff, if for no other reason than that such thinking embodies the experience of the Civil War. If Lincoln had been a Churchillian thinker, he would have conceived of employing a force to hold the main Confederate force just about where it was held for the duration of the war, between the alluring bait of Washington and the necessity of protecting Richmond for political prestige, while other Union armies overran and disrupted the economy of the area that fed and supplied it. What happened has in summary a simplicity and boldness of outline that tempts one into supposing there was a lucid inspiration and a master plan behind it. The drive down the Mississippi split the Confederacy in two, the drive on the line Nashville-Atlanta-Savannah split it into three, and as none of the three parts could sustain an army by itself the war came to an end. The further the War Between the States recedes the easier it is to see it in those terms.

The German Army's official observers of the campaigns could see none of this. They reported back at the end of the war in terms that led their newly formed Staff to adopt as a principle the doctrine that nothing of military importance can be learned from civil wars, and to form an estimate of American military competence that made them, perhaps fortunately, enormously underrate the American Army in both World Wars. The French Staff came to similar conclusions, and much of Pershing's trouble in getting his troops into the line under their own general officers in 1918 was due to deep suspicions of American command capabilities formed at Manassas and Cold Harbor and confirmed in Cuba. The British had no General Staff to take an official view of anything until after the Boer War, and by that time the crystallizing processes of history were giving the events of the Civil War a much sharper outline. The dominating problem before British military thinkers in the years after 1865 was that of a small regular army, backed by a small reserve of manpower, facing the conscription-fed mass armies of the great European powers. The problem was analogous to the one that faced the South, and the British became fascinated by the Confederacy's use of its numerically inferior forces, conceiving immense respect for Lee and something like idolatry for Stonewall Jackson. But when the British General Staff came into existence the military conception of the Empire came with it, and military writers began to seek a hero to worship who had from a central position organized an immense, widely distributed potential power as the British War Office would have to integrate the forces of the Empire. The view of the Union's military history then was that Lincoln and Stanton had muddled and confused their generals while keeping tight control of the Federal armies, but that when Grant came along and they resigned their powers to him, he gave the war a strong central direction and a coherent strategy. For a time Grant served as the hero. But on the Somme and at Arras, British military intellectuals and many others acquired a great distaste for the conception of attrition that seemed to play so important a part in Grant's thinking. As there was no alternative general to be credited with the bolder and more attractive aspects of the Federal strategy, the martial laurels were transferred to Lincoln's brow.

The newer, larger Lincoln described by Mr. Williams first saw light in an essay written in 1926 by Colin R. Ballard, a British brigadier general. It rejected the old picture of the President as a battlefield politician who had harassed and impeded his commanders with his meddling, and established him as a first-class strategist and even tactician who had again and again saved the army from itself. It rescued him, in fact, from the actual confusions and fumbles of the Civil War and set him up as a clearheaded central director who kept in mind through thick and thin a realistic strategic master plan—just the sort of man who would be needed to make the military effort of the Empire coherent and effective in the Second World War. Now that the United States has taken the place of the Empire in world affairs, it will be faced, in case of war, with the same need for a central genius to coördinate its global effort, and now Ballard's Lincoln turns up, once again, in Mr. Williams' book as an embodiment of the new necessity. Such is the process of creative evolution that makes history.

Mr. Williams, though he follows Ballard closely in his main arguments, comes to a different set of conclusions. He suggests that Lincoln divined that he was in a total war, and that he knew that he was directing a conflict not between armies but between societies. This hoists him free and clear of his age and times, and credits him with the sort of knowledge of posthumous developments that Shaw gives to Caesar. The truth seems to be that Lincoln was modern in the sense that while his generals thought the war could be won by maneuvering in and out of positions of strategic or prestige importance with a miniumum of fighting, in the manner of Marlborough and Frederick the Great, he himself thought, in the manner of Napoleon and Moltke, that it could be brought to a conclusion only by the destruction of the enemy fighting forces in battle. Mr. Williams produces no evidence that Lincoln saw the blockade, and the diffused operations all round the perimeter and in the back areas of the Confederacy, as the deadly moves against its economy that history proved them to be. He must have seen them as they were presented to him, in the only military language then spoken, as moves to cripple the Confederate armies in the field by depriving them of supplies, preventing their concentration, and inhibiting their freedom of movement. His genius was complete in its own time, just as Caesar's was. Caesar fought from the Nile Delta to the English Channel, over almost all the ground that was fought over by the Western Allies in the late war. It in no way diminishes his genius to say that he never thought of Europe as Europe, or even of the Mediterranean basin as a field for unified strategy. It in no way diminishes Lincoln's to say that he was of his time and a master of its problems and necessities; his greatness can be made to seem less than it was only by judging him in the light of needs and pressures that never weighed on him.

T. E. Lawrence

If there were no other books on the subject, Richard Aldington's biography of *Lawrence of Arabia* would be an inexplicable display of petulant denigration, but this work does not exist in isolation, and other approaches that have been made to the peculiar problem Lawrence presents do much to explain Mr. Aldington's attack, even though they cannot excuse the rancor with which it is made. The exasperating tone of these approaches, against which Mr. Aldington is in violent rebellion (the tone is a compound of mysticism and fatuity), is admirably presented in a passage from another biography of Lawrence, *The Desert and the Stars*, by Flora Armitage, in which she records the fact that, like many other human beings, the hero was born on August 16, 1888. The author then points out that Matthew Arnold had died in the previous April, that it had been an unusually wet summer, that the Parliamentary inquiry resulting from the London *Times*' articles on Parnellism and Crime was to open its hearings in the following September, and that there was trouble in the Balkans:

But one looks in vain for any augury that the child born on August 16 in that year was to be in any way unusual. Yet August 16, significantly or not, was the same day on which a hundred and nineteen years earlier the Corsican, Napoleon Bonaparte, had been born.

39

Captain Liddell Hart, the able military theorist, has written of Lawrence in a similar strain in a biographical study that was, "significantly or not," first published in March, 1934, and reprinted again and again, as often as four times in a year, through the period of the triumph of Fascism. Let us quote from the Captain's final chapter, "The Message":

Not long ago the young men were talking, the young poets writing, of him in a Messianic strain—as the man who could, if he would, be a light to lead stumbling humanity out of its troubles. It is possible that the spirit might have moved him—but not probable. And it is difficult to see any way, compatible with his philosophy, in which he could have played such a role: his indifference to "politics" was as marked as his distaste for the arts of the platform. But at least I can say that, so far as I knew him, he seemed to come nearer than any man to fitness for such power—in a state that I would care to live in. . . . For he was a message to mankind in freedom from possessiveness. In freedom from competitiveness. In freeing oneself from ambition, especially from the lust for power. His power sprang from knowledge and understanding, not from position. His influence is a living growth—because it is a spiritual message transmitting a spiritual force. The man was great; the message is greater. In him the Spirit of Freedom came incarnate to a world in fetters.

This is, of course, the rhetoric of a peroration, but Liddell Hart goes just as far in inflating the myth of Lawrence when he is supposedly soberly assessing his hero's military virtues:

Lawrence can bear comparison with Marlborough or Napoleon in that vital faculty of generalship, the power of grasping instantly the picture of the ground and situation, or relating

the one to the other, and the local to the general. . . . The
more one studies Lawrence's military career the more points of
resemblance one finds with the man who is justly regarded as
England's most representative military genius. . . . For the
truth is that Lawrence was more steeped in knowledge of war
than any of the generals of the last [1914-1918] war.

In view of the fact that Lawrence's only battle, Tafileh,
was a victory over an armed force that is said to have numbered not more than six hundred men, and that his primary
military function was to serve as liaison officer and adviser
to one of three Arab commanders whose joint armies re-
portedly amounted to twenty thousand men at the most,
this line of chatter is indeed grotesque. Mr. Aldington, who
apparently fell in love with the Regulars when he was writing a biography of the great Duke of Wellington, pursues
the matter of the fantastic lack of scale in Lawrence's sol-
dierly prowess with a feeling of outrage. In exposing the
tiny performance on which this part of the legend is based,
Mr. Aldington offers an even greater mystery. What magic
enabled Lawrence to make Liddell Hart believe in him so
completely? This brings up another question, which asks
itself even more insistently when Mr. Aldington has dipped
the whole of Lawrence's career in an acid bath of skepticism and has made an excellent case for the theory that he
was a pathological liar: Why, if he was no more than that,
did he command the respect and the interest of Winston
Churchill and Field Marshal Lord Wavell, of General Al-
lenby and Sir Ronald Storrs, of Shaw and Wells, of E. M.
Forster and Robert Graves, and of so many others? Mr.
Aldington's answer is that it was a triumph of deceit and
self-advertisement, and he would have us believe that it was
all a shabby confidence trick. But as he follows Lawrence

from birth to death and from lie to lie, the inadequacy of his reply becomes increasingly apparent. In the end there rises through the storm of Mr. Aldington's denigration a character not unlike that of Chateaubriand, in whom great qualities and gifts were combined with ruthless egotism and an insatiable appetite for admiration.

Chateaubriand's particular weakness was for the admiration of women, and he would stoop to any deception and go to any lengths to secure himself a new devotion. Lawrence did not care for women sexually, but he was incapable of meeting one without telling her that although he despised women's intellects he felt that he had at last encountered one capable of really understanding him and of entering upon a communion of minds with him as man to man. Many women found this blatant form of intellectual seduction irresistible, but their devotion was small beer for him, and usually it was a subsidiary activity on which he expended a trifling amount of his energy. The focal point of his mental life was on the business of fascinating men. Whether he was a homosexual or not is a side issue, or a very minor one. He had an obsessive, Swiftian preoccupation with and a shrinking from the physical, and the indications are that he considered sexuality as a dissipation of vital forces that could be more profitably engaged in his real business of functioning as a fascinator.

This is the key to the majority of the contradictions and discrepancies in the accounts of his thoughts and actions that Mr. Aldington has so painstakingly assembled. The secret of most successful fascinations or seductions is a simple one; the seducer not only convinces the subject that the relationship under construction is unique but also rapidly fabricates, for the purposes of the operation, a person-

ality entirely composed of answers to the subject's most
pressing necessities. Lawrence was more than just a man of
unusually delicate sensibilities; he was a chameleon, and his
rare capacity for recognizing what was required of him in
any situation was equalled only by his capacity for becoming it. In Cairo, among the intellectuals of the Arab Bureau,
he was entirely the Oxford don caught up in the war machine, ironically teasing the Regulars at G.H.Q.; in the desert with Colonel Newcombe and the fighting soldiers, he
was all plain fighting soldier; with the Arabs, all feckless
Arab, warring only when the odds were with him and when
the chance of pillage made it seem worth while; with the
Robert Graves of *Goodbye to All That*, all disillusioned
infantry officer harrowed by the darkness of war; with
Liddell Hart, the commander who had in the field arrived
at every one of Liddell Hart's tactical and strategic theories
of the indirect approach; with E. M. Forster, all sensibility
and literary intelligence; with Shaw, the ironic buffoon
indicating with a slapstick the tragic contrast between what
man knows he could do and what he does.

It is as absurd to point out in a state of moral indignation
what is irreconcilable in these various performances as it
is to point out the inconsistencies in Chateaubriand's attitudes toward the monarchy in the crises through which it
passed during his career. Chateaubriand's changing attitudes
even within the confines of a single crisis are irreconcilable,
but that is beside the point. What is to the point is that the
master egotist made each public event in which he had a
part an occasion for a dazzling display of a unique personality. If he was, in a limited sense, wicked, why, what then?
He remained Chateaubriand, and with his vivid sense of
drama he had added a brilliantly colored thread to the fabric

of his time. The same thing must be admitted of Lawrence. The ingredients of his legend are unimpressive: a career as an archeologist frustrated by the outbreak of World War I, a minor role in a great war, and then a minor role in the Royal Air Force and the Tank Corps, as a long-drawn-out substitute for suicide, after failure as a postwar *éminence grise* in Arab affairs. As a literary man, he is also dim: his major work, about the desert war, is an appendage to his public persona rather than a great book; his translation of the *Odyssey* is only fair; and *The Mint* proved, when it was published, to be an unimportant work with a few small, rude words in it, rather than the dynamic and shocking truths about military life that it had been rumored to contain. It is Saint-Exupéry and water, with its mechanic's mystique. That Lawrence was able on this small foundation to erect the image of one of the great romantic figures of his time is evidence not, as Mr. Aldington would have it, of a despicable lack of integrity but of enormous force of character. He was his own work of art, and, like Chateaubriand, he used his time as his medium for creating it. If this comparison seems too flattering to him, it may be permissible to recall the considered words of Winston Churchill, written in March, 1954: "It is the measure of his greatness that his multiple achievement has passed beyond opinion into history."

Few artists in this most exacting of fields have received a more resounding certificate of their success.

Thomas Jefferson

The Head and Heart of Thomas Jefferson, in which John Dos Passos traces Jefferson's career up to the time he resigned the office of Secretary of State, is an outstanding example of the new school of historical biography. Mr. Dos Passos has not invented a new technique but he has taken an established one farther than it has ever been taken before. The essence of the method is the exploitation of negative information, a device by which the dullest and most humdrum lives can be filled with color and movement. Mr. Dumas Malone, the author of *Jefferson and His Time,* which for all its faults is still the best biography of the man, discovered that his subject never met either Rousseau or Diderot. An earlier generation of biographers would have glumly accepted this as good reason for dropping these distinguished names from the story. But Mr. Malone was not to be daunted. He found out that Jefferson did meet an acquaintance of both men, the Baron de Grimm, and that made it possible to get them into the record:

> This oracle of society in letters and the arts might easily have introduced Jefferson to Diderot had the encyclopedist lived a few months longer. Diderot died the week before the Virginian reached Paris. Rousseau, with whom he would have had much less in common, had been dead some six years by then.

This looks like the perfection of a device for introducing irrelevant characters, but Mr. Dos Passos has invented sev-

eral improvements on it that enable him to expand the area
of irrelevance almost indefinitely. When Jefferson went to
Chiswick to see the version of the Villa Rotonda that Lord
Burlington had built there, his Lordship had been dead
thirty-three years. That does not prevent Mr. Dos Passos
from giving us an outline of his career or from telling us
who his uncle and grandfather were and what they did.

The formula for this kind of nonconnection is fairly simple. It can be expressed as: X did not meet Y, and Z was
Y's relative. But Mr. Dos Passos constructs much more
subtle chains of nonconnection, such as the one that accounts for the appearance of the actor David Garrick in the
biography. When Jefferson was a student at William and
Mary, he struck up a friendship with a Scots member of
the faculty, Dr. William Small. It is almost, though not absolutely, certain that Small had had his grounding in medicine from a Dr. John Gregory. When Gregory was himself a student, he met a dancer called Violette, and some
time after this meeting Violette married Garrick. Jefferson
never met Gregory, Small never met Violette, Gregory
never met Garrick. The pointlessness of this chain of nonconnection is made complete by the fact that Garrick died
in 1779, five years before Jefferson set foot in England.

James Watt, the inventor of the steam engine, is another
figure whom Mr. Dos Passos has succeeded in bringing into
the picture. The index shows how large a place he occupies:

Watt, James, 86, 90, 92, 94-95, 99, 131, interests Small and
Boulton in his steam engine, proposed partnership delayed by
Roebuck's claims, 282-86; early projects, 283; partnership with
Boulton finally achieved through Small, his fortune made,
286-87; explores the composition of water, invited to Paris with
Boulton, views the Machine de Marly, 287-88; 406-7, 419.

One misses the entry "meets Jefferson" for the simple reason that Watt and Jefferson never met. Small might have introduced them if he had not been dead for nine years when Jefferson came to England. Small could not mention Watt to Jefferson at William and Mary because he had not then met him. Mr. Dos Passos gives Watt all this space because Jefferson met his partner, the engineer and manufacturer Matthew Boulton. Boulton's remark to Boswell, "I sell here, Sir, what all the world desires to have—Power," shows how antipathetic his spirit was to Jefferson's; they met in an atmosphere of constraint and parted after a brief discussion limited to technical matters. This should be the end of the thing, but Mr. Dos Passos has his information about Watt on hand and is determined to use it:

Had Jefferson and Boulton met in a situation where they could talk freely, Jefferson would undoubtedly have been much stirred to learn that it was his old friend and teacher Dr. Small who had brought Boulton and Watt together.

Watt is inserted on the strength of this possibility, and then he in turn is used to drag in still more irrelevant material:

On his way home Watt stopped off for two weeks at Soho. There he found Boulton and Small the centre of a coterie of speculative spirits who visited back and forth continually between Soho and Lichfield. There was Dr. Erasmus Darwin, a big florid stammering man in a full-bottomed wig, keen on mechanical inventions, a botanist of some standing, and a poet, who turned out not only to be the grandfather of Charles Darwin, but the grandfather of the Darwinian theory. There was Keir the chemist, and two wealthy and crack-brained young men: Richard Edgeworth and Thomas Day "the philanthro-

pist" as the latter was known—whose enthusiasms and eccen-
tricities foreshadowed the romantic antics of the generation to
come. In Lichfield, at the Bishop's Palace, there were Canon
Seward's vivacious and poetical daughters, one of whom became known to fame as the Swan of Lichfield.

The construction of these links between Jefferson and the
English intelligentsia is doubly misleading, since it was his
failure to make contact with that predominantly pro-Amer-
ican middle-class section of society that accounted for his
leaving England with his already strong anti-British feelings
heightened. Almost all his English contacts were with the
King's men and members of the oligarchy, or their depend-
ents, to whom the American revolutionaries and their ideas
were unwelcome. It was precisely because he never got in
touch with Dr. Small's friends that Jefferson could not
understand Hamilton's Anglophile tendency or his readi-
ness to deal with such English pioneers of international
business as John Barker Church. They were the intelligentsia of the new manufacturing middle class, whose necessities were to create a new kind of social organization. Hamilton understood them and their necessities as Jefferson, who
derived his impressions of European social developments
largely from France, where they had not then assumed any
importance, could not. Jefferson related Hamilton's English
ideas about commerce and finance only to oligarchy and
absolutism; he had never encountered the middle class that
produced them, and he never knew of its existence. Mr.
Dos Passos quotes a letter Jefferson wrote after the War of
1812 to show his foresight in appreciating "the dreadful
price the people of England would pay for their primacy
in manufacturing in the century to come":

The population of England is composed of three descriptions of persons. . . . 1. the aristocracy, comprehending the nobility, wealthy commoners, the high grades of priesthood, and the officers of government. 2. the laboring class. 3. the eleemosynary class or paupers, who are about one fifth of the whole. The aristocracy, which have the laws and government in their hands, have so managed them as to reduce the third description below the means of supporting life, even by labor; & to force the second, whether employed in agriculture or the arts, to the maximum of labor which the construction of the human body can endure, & to the minimum of food, & of the meanest kind, which will preserve it in life.

This is actually an account of the social order dominated by the landed interest, which had been given its death blow a generation before Jefferson visited England by Sir Robert Walpole's erection of the foundations of the commercial state and by Lord Mansfield's erection of the legal basis of modern business. When Jefferson was in England, such men as Boulton, who was in reality selling power, were creating the new kind of wealth that was in the long run to reduce the aristocracy to the role of unpaid extras at such formal proceedings as coronations and royal weddings. By 1812 the social revolution was in full swing. Jefferson did not recognize that it was beginning, and considered that he was moving with the tide of the coming shape of things when he set "a dozen little boys from ten to sixteen years of age" to work making nails at Monticello. Even in 1813 he was still thinking of industrial machinery in terms of cottage craft industry, more than twenty years after Hamilton's report on manufactures had indicated where America's real wealth and strength were to come from.

Mr. Dos Passos says a good deal about Jefferson's archi-

LIBRARY

tecture while ducking away from perhaps the most revealing thing about it. Attractive as Monticello was, it was an
archaism, conceived in the most conservative Palladian-
Academic terms. When Jefferson visited Europe, he disre-
garded all the new elements in the architecture of the contemporary French and English schools, presided over by
men of the calibre of Jacques Soufflot and Robert Adam.
It was work in the style then almost fifty years behind the
times that attracted him and that he sought out. The University of Virginia buildings, in Charlottesville, which were
built to his plans and specifications in the eighteen-twenties,
produce a strange sensation of time travelling. Chronologi-
cally, the work comes after Percier and Fontaine, after such
proto-moderns as Sir John Soane and his French contemporaries Ledoux and Dubut, but in feeling it belongs back in
the world of Queen Anne, and not even in the avant-garde
of that world, for the visual connection is closer to the seventeenth-century brick Palladianism of Webb than to the
eighteenth-century stucco-and-marble Palladianism of Lord
Burlington. As one looks at those cozily dignified façades,
one realizes how much closer Jefferson was to the century
of Newton and Locke than to the nineteenth century.

Turning from the architecture to the statements of political principle and to the attacks on monarchy and aristocratic power, one sees how archaic they are, too. One
catches in Jefferson's constantly reiterated suspicions of a
powerful central government not only the tone but the
actual arguments Henry Neville had advanced in England
a century earlier in proposing a monarchy in which the
King should have no control of either the revenue or the
militia and hardly any rights, duties, or powers. And Jefferson's ideal farming state, with its home industries and small

market towns, is even closer to some of the ideas Algernon
Sidney had expressed in his *Discourses Concerning Government* late in the seventeenth century, while the second sentence of the Declaration of Independence comes, almost
entire, from pages 3 and 4 of Overton's *An Arrow Against
All Tyrants*, of 1646, along with the doctrine of the deriva-
tion of just powers from the consent of the governed. One
realizes how much more important to Jefferson what he had
read before he left America was than anything he saw in
France or England. When he came into conflict with Hamilton and the Federalists, it was—as it was when he drafted
the Declaration of Independence—the seventeenth-century
library that was his base of operations, and the section of it
given up to "the elementary books of public right, as Aris-
totle, Cicero, Locke, Sidney, etc." Until he learned politics
in Washington's Cabinet, it was his meetings with these
people that were the vital events of his life, and an account
of his early years has to concern itself with them. Mr. Dos
Passos mentions Sidney four times but never says what his
ideas were, though they are certainly more important than,
say, the list of liquor prices set by the Goochland County
justices when Jefferson was two, or the lists of game shot
on a surveying trip in which he (aged seven) took no part.
But it is the mode for the hair-tidy school of scholarship to
concern itself with such things, and to present these "color-
ful" combings as germane to the heads and hearts of great
men while the true substance of their lives and their greatness goes into the discard on the ground that it is too difficult or too dull for the general reader.

Alfred de Vigny

Alfred de Vigny, the author of *The Military Necessity*, published a hundred and twenty years after it was written, is a fascinating figure in the literary world, an essentially minor French writer whose reputation has been inflated by generation after generation of critics until he now occupies a position of considerable importance as a forerunner of the modern literary movement. Picking one's way through the verse and the prose of de Vigny, detail by detail, one comes on magnificent things, such as the enormously evocative line from his poem "Le Cor" that embodies the whole flavor of the French romantic movement: *"Dieu! que le son du cor est triste au fond des bois."* The evocation is immediate and inescapable; one sees the melancholy figure of the poet, emotionally disturbed, Byronic, and apart, leaning against a tree, beaver hat in hand, looking at the misty autumn landscape of a genteel park and hearing the faint tootling of a hunting horn in a covert in the middle distance. In fact, though, the horn which evokes this line is the horn of the Song of Roland, and it is desperately at the lips of the trapped hero overwhelmed by the Saracens and by black-hearted treachery in the gorge of Roncevaux. De Vigny has given one of the great stories of heroism and action a languid, fin-de-siècle melancholy.

Another of his anthology lines is, on the face of it, a

splendid statement of the stoic ideal. How should one die? In silence, without weakness.

> *Comment on doit quitter la vie et tous ses maux,*
>   *C'est vous qui le savez. . . .*
> *Seul le silence est grand; tout le reste est faiblesse.*

Something dignified is being said about a good death, but the poem, "La Mort du Loup," is about a soundly monogamous wolf who makes the supreme sacrifice in defense of his wife and family, and as a pin for that particular idea it is not far short of being ridiculous.

A good deal of de Vigny's repute as a forerunner rests on his interest in the problem of evil. The poem that is explicitly about this subject, "Eloa," stands up as long as one talks in generalities about its subject, but not if one examines its actual content. Eloa is a lady angel whose gently sentimental heart is filled with curiosity about Satan and his wickedness. Perhaps, she dreams, the influence of a really good woman could save him from himself. Satan is, as it happens, remarkably good-looking as well as remarkably wicked, and before long poor Eloa is snugly in his arms inside a cloud of flame that serves him as a bachelor apartment and also as a kind of elevator. While it carries the pair of them down to Hell, Eloa pesters Satan with increasingly banal questions and gets increasingly sullen answers from the demon:

> "*Seras-tu plus heureux du moins, es-tu content?*"
> "*Plus triste que jamais.*"

If the poem is really the forerunner of anything, it is the forerunner of those novels by Marie Corelli and Ethel M. Dell in which evil is personified by saturnine persons who own yachts and look good in evening dress.

In 1826, a couple of years after the publication of "Eloa," de Vigny met Walter Scott and was inspired by the incident to produce a best-seller, *Cinq-Mars*, a cloak, sword, and cleavage novel, dealing with the intrigues of the Cardinal de Richelieu, in which a good deal is cribbed from Scott's *Quentin Durward* but not improved. Better writers than de Vigny have written worse books than *Cinq-Mars*, but the peculiarly disorganized quality of his mind is shown by the fact that when he published this complete travesty of history and psychology he added, by way of preface, an essay, "Thoughts on Truth in Art," that was very absolute indeed in its demand for *la vérité d'observation sur la nature humaine*. It is as if Mr. T. S. Eliot, having written *Anthony Adverse* or something of the kind, decided to publish it in conjunction with one of his more austere essays.

With this schizoid performance, de Vigny began to hit his stride. He had been an officer in the French Army for thirteen years, and he now wangled a series of leaves of absence and, finally, a discharge on medical grounds, so that he could write for the theatre. Edmund Kean's visit to Paris in 1828 with an English company to play a Shakespeare season excited de Vigny just as his meeting with Scott had excited him, and within the following twelve months he ran off translations of *The Merchant of Venice*, *Romeo and Juliet*, and *Othello*. The last, entitled *Le More de Venise*, was turned out with breakneck speed for the express purpose of beating Victor Hugo's *Hernani* out for a place in the schedule of the Théâtre Français, an aim in which he was successful. His grasp of theatrical realities and his hardheaded professional approach showed themselves again, a little later, after the near disaster of the first night of Dumas's *Christine*. De Vigny and Hugo began working over the play at one in the morning, and had a revised version ready for rehearsal at noon the next day.

De Vigny, by this time a husband, found a mistress in the theatre—the Marie Dorval whom George Sand described as "*Oh! naïve et passionnée, et jeune et suave, et tremblante et terrible.*" The relationship between the two ladies was ambiguous, but there was no doubt about her relationship with Dumas. She had begun her affair with him by popping her head out of a cab window at one in the morning and saying, "Come inside and kiss me." From then on, she referred to Dumas as her "big bow-wow." She had been on the stage for ten years when de Vigny met her, and she was an accomplished sexual athlete who both amused herself and furthered her career by taking her pleasure where she found it. Edmund Gosse rather misleadingly refers to the liaison she and de Vigny set up as a seraphic and mystical one, and compares it to that of a nun and her brother. As she was unfaithful to him all the time, and he was untrue to her when she was on tour in the provinces, the comparison seems a poor one.

What is most interesting about this phase of de Vigny's career is that it led to his writing *Stello*, an argument in the form of a story which defines the place of the poet in society. It is a powerful statement of the theory that the artist belongs in the ivory tower and not in the market place. Solitary and free, he must keep himself to himself, unspotted by the world, clear of all mundane ambitions and vulgar interests. While he was writing this, de Vigny was deep in intrigues to get the lead in his play *La Maréchale d'Ancre* for Marie Dorval, and after it was produced he wrote another play, *Quitte pour la Peur*, simply to provide her with a star part.

De Vigny was now at the height of his popularity, and, like Victor Hugo and Dumas, a force in the French theatre. His next play, called *Chatterton*, was based on *Stello*. It declared that poets were social outcasts and that to possess genius was to inherit the curse of Cain. It was typical of de Vigny that he chose as his exemplar of genius Thomas Chatterton, a light versifier without any inventive gift, who committed suicide after he had been exposed as the author of some poems which he had presented as the work of a fifteenth-century poet, named Rowley, a wholly imaginary character. It was typical, too, that de Vigny pointed to neglect and indifference as the danger to the poet at a time when society was raising its altars to the bitch goddess success and threatening its geniuses with too much money, too much worship, and too little time to think, see, and feel. (This new situation was summed up by the reply Tennyson got from a manufacturer when he tried to buy some barbed wire—"I could not think of making any charge, for, if I may say it without taking a liberty, the honour of having your Lordship's name on the firm's books . . . is in itself ample payment.") There was real danger that poets would be fattened like Strasbourg geese and a smooth, expensive paste made out of their sensibilities.

Chatterton was followed by *Servitude et Grandeur Militaires*, published here as *The Military Necessity*. De Vigny had been a poor officer, who despised his superiors and antagonized them by courting popularity among his subordinates. It is one thing in military circles to be a G.I.s' general; it is quite another thing to be a G.I.s' lieutenant. His literary interests made him indifferent to his duties, and although he had influential friends in the government throughout his military career, he received only one promotion in his thirteen years of service. When he felt like leaving the Army for the theatre, he left it. Mr. Humphrey Hare, in an introduction to *The Military Necessity*, admirably states the book's argument:

The army is more than an occupation, more than a profession; it is a way of life, a dedication. Within its ranks there is room neither for the undisciplined enthusiasm of the volunteer nor the impotent reluctance of the conscript. They are merged in the common mold of discipline, become indistinguishable in the uniform of abnegation. And this personal surrender to a dedicated way of life has, like every mystery, its visible signs and ceremonies. The donning of the vestments by the priest, the sacred dance before the altar, the chanting of the ritual are at once the symbols of initiation and a rhythmic, almost hypnotic, control of the physical which must precede all essential spiritual experience. So it is with the soldier: his uniform, his music, and his drill are all means to an arcane ideal, the state of military grace. They set him apart, mark him as a member of a dedicated sect.

De Vigny declares this elevated mystique in *The Military Necessity* in the course of presenting three short stories that one can only call ludicrous melodramas. The first is the story of the captain of a Navy brig under the Directory, who sails to Cayenne with a charming young couple aboard as passengers and sealed orders, not to be opened until his ship has crossed latitude one between the twenty-seventh and twenty-eighth parallels. When this point is reached, he opens the paper and discovers that he has to shoot the young husband, of whom he is now a firm friend. He does his duty, and the young woman goes out of her mind. The captain, in disgust, transfers to the Army and spends the next eighteen years rising to the rank of battalion com-

mander as he fights his way through Napoleon's campaigns.
Everywhere he goes, he takes the poor lunatic lady with
him in what sounds like a miniature prairie schooner. The
second story is about the royal kindness of Marie Antoi-
nette, and it would be ungracious to comment on it in the
face of the innocent enthusiasms of a Coronation year. The
third is concerned with drawing a contrast between the
saintly mysticism of Vice-Admiral Lord Collingwood and
the vulgarity of Napoleon Bonaparte.

The question is why anyone should take these rigmaroles
and their fantastic mystique seriously, and the answer is
extremely simple. De Vigny was incapable of writing an
ugly sentence, and every minor incident, every digression,
in which he creates the atmosphere and background of his
nonsense, shines like a jewel. The episodes in which de
Vigny as general narrator meets with the narrators of the
three stories have a perfection as intimate descriptive writing that has been equalled only by Turgenev in his *Sports-
man's Sketches*, and the conclusion of the second story, in
which its narrator is killed when the magazine of a fortress
blows up, is so fine in its tranquil observation of violence
that one can almost accept de Vigny's ensuing remarks on
the nobility and devotion to duty of the victim and disregard the fact that it is his gross negligence that has caused
the disaster.

The book's history is fascinating. It was considered an
attack on the Army when it first appeared, and was not
popular until after the French defeat of 1870. Then its
doctrine of the dedicated life of self-abnegation took hold
of those intellectual officers who, devoted to the destruction
of the Third Republic, were making themselves a third
force in French politics. The mystique of absolute surren-

der to the Army and its higher national purposes justified
the conspirators of the War Office in their long fight to
maintain the fiction of the infamy of Dreyfus. The question
of his guilt or innocence was unimportant; he had sinned
against the Army by invoking civil justice, a monstrous
crime in one who had put on the uniform and forsaken the
world.

The latter stages of the career of the inventor of the
aesthetic of the ivory tower are sad. Not long after he published *Servitude et Grandeur Militaires*, he discovered the
full extent of Marie Dorval's iniquity. He had, with some
bitterness, forgiven her George Sand, but he could not forgive her Dumas. Shocked by her treachery, he withdrew
from the theatre and returned to his wife, an Englishwoman
whom he had married in 1825. After four years of caustic
reflection, he produced *La Colère de Samson*. It was a
memorable explosion, with a strong tang of Mauriac in its
view of woman:

> *Toujours voir serpenter la vipère dorée*
> *Qui se traîne en sa fange et s'y croit ignorée!*
> *Toujours ce compagnon dont le cœur n'est pas sûr,*
> *La Femme, enfant malade et douze fois impur!*

Soon after, the advocate of solitude and abstention from
worldly affairs for artists was putting forward his candida-
ture for the Academy, and after six tries, and endless in-
trigue and maneuver, he made it in 1845. In 1848, he ran
for the Legislative Assembly, and in 1852, after the Bona-
partist coup, he angled for the post of French Ambassador
to London, without success. He spent his remaining years
assiduously attending the meetings of the Academy and
carping delicately on the margins of things.

In spite of the beauty of his language, which can make even rubbish like *Cinq-Mars* worth reading, there is no way of treating de Vigny as anything but a comedian. He was pursued by fate, but it always made farce out of his tragic situations. His marriage would have been unbearably sad if he had been another kind of man. He married a beautiful woman, all gold, pink, and blue. This golden girl was a goose whose malapropisms became famous in de Vigny's circle; she would say "as proud as Luther" and confuse such words as "exclude" and "include" in her muddled talk. Her father, Sir Hugh Mills Bunbury, supposedly immensely rich, with sugar plantations in Demerara, cut them off with a tiny allowance. She became an invalid soon after the marriage and was bedridden for long periods from then until her death. One is prepared to pity the young couple and to hate the wicked Sir Hugh. But de Vigny chose to console himself with Marie Dorval and to make himself a figure of fun. And Sir Hugh (who was not really, as it turned out, very rich) was addlepated rather than wicked, and soon simply forgot about his daughter and son-in-law. When, only two years later, Bunbury met Lamartine, who was honeymooning in Florence, he was struck by the coincidence that his own daughter was married to a French poet. "But which?" Sir Hugh wondered. He could no longer remember.

Fate endowed de Vigny with almost every gift that would make him a stricken genius of the romantic movement and give him a place in the history of letters alongside Chénier, Keats, and Shelley. But it failed to give him the substance that would withstand a blow. It is perhaps no accident that he chose Chatterton as his hero.

Harriette Wilson

The Game of Hearts is that old friend of the collector of erotic literature, *The Memoirs of Harriette Wilson*, now skillfully edited by Lesley Blanch and also enriched by her with an introductory biographical and explanatory essay. The explanation for the editing of the memoirs is not the one that first leaps to the mind; it has its origins in a subtler region. Miss Wilson, an English lady of carefree disposition (three of her sisters were of the same profession), practiced her simple arts upon mankind during the sunlit afterglow of the age of reason, in the first two decades of the nineteenth century, and then descended to reminiscence in the inflamed dawn of Romanticism. The effect of this period on her writing was considerable, and unfortunate. She had approached love in the spirit in which the young approach tennis today; she liked a hard, fast game and an opponent who required no concessions. Her appetites were simple, and simply satisfied. As a starter, she lent herself with enthusiasm, and at an early age, to her seduction by the young son of a washerwoman from Hammersmith, the riverside suburb of London where she was brought up. He made his living rowing a wherry—a sort of water taxi—on the Thames, and her romance with him fitted in with her sister Amy's affair with a muscular miller who lived upstream at Isleworth; for their sessions of pleasure, the wherryman would row the two girls up to snug moorings among the

61

willow-fringed water meadows along the river. Harriette's feelings for the oarsman were uncomplex; she appreciated him robustly as "a lusty, carroty lad, with the finest set of teeth I ever saw." Her feelings for men did not change. She lost one protector after another because she could not resist the attractions of any fine physical specimen who happened along. And she finally ruined herself by leaving the son of the Duke of Beaufort, Lord Worcester, who had her in keeping on a more or less permanent basis at forty pounds a month, the use of his carriage, and a handsome apartment, for a man called Meyler. She decided to have Meyler the moment he was described to her:

"No woman can do anything with Meyler, in the way of love," said Sir John; "for Meyler really don't know what sentiment means. . . . Meyler is a mere animal, a very handsome one, it is true, and there is much natural shrewdness about him, besides that he is one of the most gentlemanlike young men I know; but you may read his character in his countenance."

"What is that like?" I asked.

"It is beautiful," said Sir John Boyd, "and so peculiarly voluptuous that, when he looks at women, after dinner, although his manner is perfectly respectful, they are often observed to blush deeply, and hang down their heads, they really cannot tell why or wherefore."

Meyler was, in short, a peach Harriette Wilson was determined to pluck; she thought and acted in these matters like an eighteenth-century rake. But by the time she found herself in straitened circumstances, her looks lost, fighting to hold a handsome bully called Rochfort, and reduced to the writing of her memoirs as a desperate expedient for raising money, the fashion in sentiment had changed. The great characters of romantic fiction—Chateaubriand's René, Goethe's Werther, and Lord Byron's Lord Byron—had cast their shadows across every couch and double bed; the age of brisk amorousness had given way to that of emotional *Sturm und Drang*. Miss Wilson, who had trimmed her memoirs down by omitting her recollections of several gentlemen in return for substantial cash payments, felt obliged to fatten them by inserting no end of romantic fiddledeedee about the depth of her passions. This playful wit and amorist, who had charmed her way to the top of her exacting profession by the use of her candor and high spirits (she was not possessed of exceptional good looks), in consequence became a good deal of a bore, giving the impression of being at once intolerably long-winded and profoundly dishonest. Her book, after a *succès de scandale* won by its anecdotes about the Duke of Wellington and the members of the Whig aristocracy, was consigned to the obscure domain of "curious" literature, being reprinted in successively dingier editions for successively smaller publics. And since it contains nothing pornographic, it disappointed these new publics even more keenly than its other publics. Miss Lesley Blanch has ably revitalized the memoirs and, by cutting away the wadding and the fraudulent romanticism, has created a book that fully lives up to the promise of this spanking opening:

I shall not say why and how I became, at the age of fifteen, the mistress of the Earl of Craven. Whether it was love, or the severity of my father, the depravity of my own heart, or the winning arts of the noble Lord, which induced me to leave my paternal roof and place myself under his protection, does not now much signify.

Harriette Wilson is thus off at a hand gallop. The Earl of Craven, a military man, made the mistake of fighting his battles again on paper to pass away his hours with Harriette in their apartment on the Marine Parade, in Brighton. Accordingly, she first flirted with the Honourable Frederick Lamb, Lord Melbourne's son, and was finally put out of Craven's door after being surprised on the lap of his West Indian footman, Mungo. It was then Lamb's turn, but he did not last, either.

I discovered, on our arrival in London, that he was a voluptuary, somewhat worldly and selfish. My comforts were not considered. I lived in extreme poverty, while he contrived to enjoy all the luxuries of life; and suffered me to pass all my evenings alone, while he frequented balls, masquerades, etc. . . . I felt that I deserved better from him.

This feeling—or, rather, a feeling that she deserved better from someone—led her to write a note informing the Marquis of Lorne that if he were to walk up Duke's Row, Somerstown, he would meet a most lovely girl. And so it was Lorne's turn. But Harriette was now well known, and, while noble lords thronged nightly to her doors, she was soon set for one of the biggest successes of her career. The ground was prepared for her liaison with the almost excessively handsome Lord Ponsonby, by a kind friend of Harriette who explained the situation to her in terms that adequately sum up the morals and attitudes of the Whig society of the time. Ponsonby had married Lady Jersey's sixteen-year-old daughter Fanny after that young lady had been struck stone-deaf and had lost half her wits and all her hair during a violent attack of scarlet fever:

He [Ponsonby] felt the deepest interest, admiration, and pity for her. He considered, with horror, the bare possibility of this sweet, fragile, little being becoming the wife of some man who might, hereafter, treat her harshly . . . so, to secure her from any of these evils, he resolved to propose for her himself. I need not add, that he was joyfully accepted, by both mother and daughter. He might have done better, and I fancy Ponsonby sometimes wishes that his wife could be his friend and companion; but that is quite out of the question. Her Ladyship is good, and will do as she is bid; but besides her deafness, her understanding is neither bright nor lively. Lord Ponsonby shews her the sort of indulgence and tenderness which a child requires; but he must seek for a companion elsewhere.

Having established herself as Ponsonby's secret companion, Harriette might have made herself secure for life, but she was incapable of either fidelity or discretion. She flaunted the connection until it came to Fanny Ponsonby's knowledge. Since Harriette was already flagrantly unfaithful to her protector, Ponsonby was probably relieved when his wife won his promise to break with the mistress who was making him appear ridiculous.

After a raffish interlude of transient affairs, Harriette negotiated an understanding with Lord Worcester. She might have taken this one no more seriously than all her others if an extraordinary success of her younger sister Sophia had not suggested the possibility of a greater coup. Sophia's success involved Worcester's uncle, Lord William Somerset, who was what was called a tiger, one of those mysterious forerunners of the modern sports-car set, a man devoted to rapid motion, whose sole passion in life was performing the functions of a coachman and setting up new records for the run from London to Brighton or London to Bath. He had a singular arrangement with a Lord Berwick, which Harriette describes laconically:

Viscount Berwick was a nervous, selfish, odd man, and afraid to drive his own horses. Lord William Somerset was an excellent whip; but he had no horses to whip. Lord Berwick, like Lord Barrymore, wanted a tiger; while Somerset required a man whose curricle he could drive, and whose money he could borrow. The bargain was struck; and Tiger Somerset had driven Lord Berwick some years, when His Lordship, after having for more than a fortnight been looking at my sister Sophia, at her window, one day addressed the tiger as follows:

"I have, at last, found a woman I should like to marry, Somerset, and you know I have been more than twenty years upon the lookout."

Somerset effected the necessary introduction, and before long Sophia was Lady Berwick, married in style at St. George's, in Hanover Square, and installed in no mere kept woman's apartment but in the full legal splendor of her husband's house in Grosvenor Square. This triumph aroused Harriette, the more so as Berwick made his wife, now respectable, drop her notorious sister. The Marquis of Worcester, the heir to the dukedom of the Beauforts and the great Badminton estate, was an even finer catch than Berwick, and would, if Harriette could manage it, establish her on an even higher social level. Worcester was infatuated, and there is little doubt that she could have brought a marriage off. But her old incapacity for fidelity tripped her again; it was at this point that the beautiful Mr. Meyler, a slightly raffish man-about-town, came to her attention, and she also had passades with rankers when she was in rooms in the towns where Worcester was stationed with his regiment. Worcester recovered from his infatuation, and his father, the Duke of Beaufort, who had agreed to pay her the equivalent of a modern ten thousand dollars a year, conditional on her not getting married to his son, was able to evade this agreement.

Meyler was a savage bully, as well as a sensualist, and his chief claim to fame is that he ruined Beau Brummell. He acquired the name of the Dandy-Killer by standing all one morning in the lobby of White's Club telling every member who came in the details of a dishonorable swindle Brummell had tried to bring off. Brummell left England, but Meyler's act was a breach of the conventions of that generation's *louche* gambling, womanizing society, and it made him an ambiguous figure. Harriette's association with him at this dangerous phase of her career was fatal. When Meyler broke with her, she had a seedy interlude in Paris, and then at last met her doom on a visit to London. She was picked up on the street by a Colonel Rochfort, whose rank was as bogus as his claim to be the wronged heir to an Irish earldom. She paid his debts in order to get him to marry her, and afterward wrote her memoirs to support him in the manner to which he was accustomed. Little is known of her after a police-court episode of 1829 in which she had some difficulty raising bail; she vanishes from sight with the tables turned—she is keeping a man.

Harriette Wilson's book is a valuable corrective to some of the recent attempts to present English society of the Regency as all elegance, common sense, and rationality about sex, for it creates an unforgettable impression of the age's not inconsiderable and just as characteristic raw and harum-scarum side, but a word of caution is necessary. The author is reliable only in suggesting the kind of thing that went on; she cannot be relied upon for facts. She wrote as freely as she lived, and one of the best things in the book is a description of the death of a woman she disliked—Julia Johnstone, a colleague, who was thoroughly alive at the time and who subsequently wrote a commentary on Harriette's memoirs. Miss Lesley Blanch has had the happy thought of inserting extracts from this commentary at points in the book where corrections are plainly necessary. She has also added an amusing anecdotal biographical index of Harriette's victims, and an essay on the social background of her activities. This includes, among other good things, the story of a Miss Rachel Lee, who was kidnapped in a post chaise by two gentlemen, one of them a clergyman of the Church of England. When her assailants were put on trial for rape, it emerged, in the cross-examination of the injured party, that on finding herself inside the carriage she had torn a small camphor bag from her breast, saying, "The charm that has hitherto preserved my virtue is dissolved! Now welcome pleasure!" The gentlemen were thereupon acquitted, amid cheers from the public. It is a mistake to apply moral judgments to such an age; one can only take the aspect of it described in Harriette Wilson's memoirs as dispassionately as Jane Austen took another of its aspects in the novel she wrote when she was a girl—*Jack and Alice*:

The Masks were then all removed and the Company retired to another room, to partake of an elegant and well managed Entertainment, after which the Bottle being pretty briskly pushed about by the 3 Johnsons, the whole party not excepting even Virtue were carried home, Dead Drunk.

It is not that Jane Austen was condoning vice or immorality; she was writing as a child in a tough society, and with a child's exemplary calm. Harriette writes with the same calm about her career; one sees that she remained what she was when the wherryman found her, a physically precocious child, and all that one can say of her in the way of moral judgment is that she was a greedy one.

Florence Nightingale

The subject of the biography *Florence Nightingale*, by Cecil Woodham-Smith, exists in the minds of such people as think of her at all either as the sentimental stereotype summed up by the phrase "the lady with the lamp"—the merciful, cool-handed angel of the Crimean hospitals—or as the absurd, crusading do-gooder of Lytton Strachey's essay in *Eminent Victorians*, the termagant who hounded poor, indolent Sydney Herbert to his grave with her demoniac energy and who, having outlined the right path for everything on earth, set out at last to outline reforms for Heaven. Since, on the published record, Florence Nightingale's lifework was centered on drains and sanitation, and her principal achievements were the reform of hospital hygiene and the foundation of the modern system of training and disciplining nurses, the temptation to go to any trouble to probe for the real woman behind the myths is readily resistible. The record is inadequate and wholly misleading; Florence Nightingale was one of the most remarkable women of her time, and her story is both fascinating and moving. Strachey badly underestimated her, because he was writing too close to her. *Eminent Victorians* was published in 1918, only eight years after her death, and before her family was ready to yield up its secrets or hers. The intervening years have removed all those who might have been hurt, and an immense amount of material, which is far richer in interest than anyone could have foreseen, has been made available to Mrs. Woodham-Smith. Florence Nightingale felt unable to confide in anyone during her childhood, and at a very early stage she formed a habit, which lasted all her life, of releasing her bottled-up feelings and secret opinions by putting them on paper, in notes that varied in length from a single line to several hundred words. What emerges from these notes, all fortunately preserved, is a unique history of emotional development and mystical experience.

The Nightingale family situation was typically Victorian, as complex and overplotted as the contemporaneous three-decker novel. Florence should have been a boy. Her very wealthy father, William Edward, had only a life interest in his property. If he died without a male heir, it went to his sister, and then to any male issue she might have. When he was twenty-four, William Edward married a woman of thirty whom he had known since his childhood and who until then had shown a marked preference for men a good deal older than herself. She produced first one daughter, Parthenope, and then another, Florence. There were to be no more children, and as this fact became clear, William Edward's sister produced the man-child who would ultimately disinherit them. The eleven-year-old Florence, with a child's intuition for the deadly spot, exasperated her mother by developing an extravagant and unbalanced devotion for the little boy. Her father made trouble for everyone by settling down to give the girls a male education. As no governess could be found capable of giving them more than the namby-pamby female equipment of the piano, water colors, and so forth, he taught them himself— Greek, Latin, German, French, Italian, history, and philos-

ophy. His elder daughter rebelled against her education
and fled whenever she could to her mother's purely feminine world of family gossip and chatter. Florence stayed
with it and became not only a brilliant student but also
very much her father's friend. When he wanted to reprove
his silly, girlish elder daughter, he made his criticisms to
Florence, to be passed on. A hostility that lasted until death
grew up between the two girls.

This hotbed of Freudian tensions would have produced
trouble at any time, but the eighteen-thirties were ideal for
its development. The romantic vogue for sensibility was at
its height; intemperate Wertheresque language, passionate
declarations, scenes, and fantods with smelling salts were
the order of the day. There was no escape from the physical
and emotional trap. Ladies were ladies, and purely orna-
mental. William Edward Nightingale was a gentleman and
would have injured his social standing had he ever worked
at anything; he never did a hand's turn, and nobody ever
thought he should. After one political venture, from which
he emerged unsuccessful and disgusted, he found refuge in
the world of abstract speculation, where he pursued such
nebulosities as the nature of moral impulses, the relations
of ethics to aesthetics, and proof of the immortality of the
soul. The life open to Florence, with the man's mind her
father gave her, was summed up by a friend of hers, in the
nonsense talk that so many British Victorians used as a
code to express their inner bitterness: "Faddling, twaddling,
and the endless tweedling of nosegays in jugs."

The situation was all the more intolerable because the
social world in which the family lived was superficially
ultracivilized. When such people as Ranke, the historian,
and the Chevalier Bunsen, the Prussian Ambassador and one

of the foremost European Egyptologists, came to dine with the Nightingales, it would be to meet the best of English society: Lord Palmerston, the Foreign Secretary; Lord Ashley, the reformer; and so on. Florence was invited to house-parties at such places as Chatsworth, the vast palace of the Duke of Devonshire, and introduced to members of the Royal Family. Richard Monckton Milnes, son of a wealthy landowner, editor of the first collected edition of Keats' works, and the most promising young politician of the day, was devoted to her and was pressing her to marry him. But there was no place in this society for her to be anything but a woman and a noodle. Monckton Milnes' devotion could only bind her to another version of the same stultifying life, to faddling and twaddling in another house. If the story were only a matter of a pioneer feminist in a man's world, the story of her attempts to break out—against the fury and resentment of her father and mother, and despite the unremitting emotional blackmail of her sister— it would be interesting enough. But the nature of the girl's motivations in breaking out gives it an unusual fascination.

Strachey made heavy-handed fun of the naïveté of Florence Nightingale's religious ideas, teasing her in one passage about having a relationship with God rather too like her relationship with Sydney Herbert. "One has the impression," wrote Strachey, "that Miss Nightingale has got the Almighty too into her clutches, and that, if He is not careful, she will kill Him with over-work." It turns out that this was her own sort of joke about herself: "I MUST remember God is not my private secretary." It would be just possible for a certain kind of literalist to have written this seriously; Florence Nightingale, however, was anything but that, and could jeer at some aspects of conventional religion from a standpoint not far removed from Strachey's own. She summarized the books of Samuel and Kings as "Witches. Harlots. Talking Asses. Asses Talking. Young Gentlemen caught by the Hair. Savage Tricks. Priests' Tales." When she attempted to describe her God, it was as the Absolute, Perfection, or Truth—as a universal mind fairly closely resembling the concept of God that Einstein owned to. She had a logically bewildering relationship with this concept; it was one that forcefully demonstrates the wide gulf separating the mystic from the average person. Her cosmic Absolute could, and did, speak to her directly, in a human voice, without even the messenger angels through whom Joan of Arc's simpler God spoke to her. The relationship was the reverse of the one imagined by Strachey, and it is characteristic of it that when, in Athens, she was overtaken by a crisis of belief, she did not go to any church or chapel to pray but sought out the cave in the rock of the Acropolis sacred to the Eumenides, the relentless Furies of the old Greek faith.

The strange thing about Florence Nightingale's call, so difficult for the modern mind to comprehend, is that it ordered her into the modern world, and not out of it. The result of her mystical experience was to make her a creative force in the shaping of a professional outlook in matters of hospital administration. When she finally escaped from her family into the Crimean hospitals, she found herself fighting an amateur system of administration, wholly eighteenth century in its practice and thought. She arrived on the scene as the embodiment of modern ideas. The medieval religious nursing orders had long before disintegrated. The nurse of the time was a prostitute too old for work, a drunk unemployable in any other capacity, or, at best, a doctor's or medical student's doxy. The whole contemporary hospital system was in tune with its nurses; hospitals were not places where people were taken to get well but places where the poor were taken to die. The hospital she took over at Scutari was a Dachau—a huge Turkish barracks, dilapidated and with a leaking roof, in which the wounded were laid on the floor in rows. Here there were no nurses at all, only untrained orderlies. The sanitation, since the existing toilets were unspeakable and unapproachable, consisted of huge tubs set between the rows of sick men. The water supply passed through a conduit partly blocked by the carcass of a dead horse. There was no breakdown of administration to account for these things; it had simply never occurred to anyone that such matters needed planning. That all this was the norm of less than a century ago is an astonishing reminder of the novelty of the ideas of fundamental decency that one accepts unthinkingly as part of the Western tradition.

What Florence Nightingale created from the horror of the Crimea was the instrument for the care of the sick without which nineteenth-century progress in surgery and bacteriology would have been meaningless. A Marxist would deem it historic necessity; she heard it as the voice of God. When she returned from the Crimea, she continued her work with the creation of a civilian nursing body, but a twist of circumstances carried her influence into another field. She was asked to make suggestions for improving the health of the British Army in India. This led inevitably to suggestions for improving the sanitation of towns where the Army had its stations. And this, in turn, led to the first modern statistical inquiry into public health by a British government department, and it is not too much to say

that it led, in the long run, to the reform of the whole
Indian administration along professional lines. Her insistent,
scolding, demanding voice became the voice of the modern
world expressing its dissatisfaction with an obsolete technique of government. There is a certain symbolic perfection in her hounding to death poor Sydney Herbert, who
had been Secretary of War at the beginning of the Crimean
campaign and who later became Chairman of the Royal
Commission on the Health of the Army in India, by her
demands that he reform his department. What she was
hounding to death was the amateur, the gentleman aesthete
born to power, the type figure of a ruling class that the
world had outgrown.

This gracefully written and extremely readable biography has the power and intensity of a fine novel. It is also
a first-class contribution to social history, for it gives an
extraordinary insight into the strengths and weaknesses of
the British and their Empire in the nineteenth century. It
establishes Florence Nightingale as one of the really remarkable human beings of history—the comparison that
suggests itself more and more compellingly as one reads
is with Gandhi—and it is a revelation of the strange and
obscure sources of human greatness.

Monckton Milnes

The name of the subject of Mr. James Pope-Hennessy's richly anecdotal two-volume biography, *Monckton Milnes*, is likely to be familiar only to the more attentive readers of *The Education of Henry Adams*. Henry Adams was glad to accept an invitation to a weekend at Monckton Milnes' country house, at Fryston, in Yorkshire, in December of 1862, because his host was one of the few upper-class Englishmen he had encountered who supported the cause of the North, and it was a relief to escape for a few days from the coldness of largely pro-Confederate London society. When he came away from Fryston, he was more than glad he had gone, because he had been a guest for some days in a house that contained one of the best libraries in England and because he had enjoyed the company of a brilliant talker and a funny writer, Laurence Oliphant, who had just returned from Japan, but most of all because he had met the poet Swinburne:

. . . and there after dinner all sat—or lay—till far into the night, listening to the rush of Swinburne's talk. In a long experience, before or after, no one ever approached it; yet one had heard accounts of the best talking of the time, and read accounts of the best talkers in all time, among the rest, of Voltaire, who seemed to approach nearest the pattern.

As he listened with delight to intellectual conversation so unlike, in tone and content, what he had heard from

Lowell and Emerson in Concord and Boston, the shy young man of twenty-four was aware that his education was being extended. He was also acute enough to be aware that his host knew it, and he was delighting vicariously in his host's experience. He shrewdly put his finger on a leading trait of Milnes' character:

Commonly country visits are much alike, but Monckton Milnes was never like anybody, and his country parties served his purpose of mixing strange elements. Fryston was one of a class of houses that no one sought for its natural beauties . . . so that the singular guests whom Milnes collected to enliven his December had nothing to do but astonish each other, if anything could astonish such men.

Milnes was indeed an artist in social astonishments, and some of his effects, which Mr. Pope-Hennessy describes in detail in his biography, are among the great achievements of their kind. At Eastertide of 1863 he built a little house-party around the Archbishop of York, the novelist Thackeray, his daughter Anne, and her younger sister. Part of the conversation Friday night was devoted to preparing the ground for the appearance of the charming, the delightful, the gifted young Swinburne. He appeared, as advertised, the following day, in the full flower of his considerable beauty. Anne Thackeray, recalling the incident for the benefit of Edmund Gosse, said that Swinburne seemed to her "like Apollo or a fairy prince" as he joined the party, walking across a lawn "swinging his hat in his hand, and letting the sunshine flood the bush of his red-gold hair." Swinburne charmed the men with his intellectual powers and the girls with his playfulness, and all went swimmingly until Sunday evening, when, after dinner, Monckton Milnes pressed Swinburne to read some of his poems. He opened strongly with "The Leper" and then proceeded to "Les Noyades," a poem vividly setting forth the sufferings of two young persons who are punished, after being detected in illicit amour, by being lashed together face to face and thrown into a river. The Archbishop was saved from apoplexy by the arrival of the butler, who flung open the drawing-room doors to announce that it was time for family prayers. The servants then joined the party for that now obsolete form of divine worship.

Another of Milnes' little coups of social terrorism occurred in May of 1848, the year of revolution. He was staying, Mr. Pope-Hennessy tells us, at the Hotel Meurice, in Paris, witnessing with excited pleasure the turmoil that followed the flight of King Louis Philippe and the establishment of the Second Republic. "Dinner at home," he noted in his commonplace journals, with pussycat restraint: "G. Sand, Mr. and Mrs. Conyngham, Tocqueville, Mérimée, de Vigny, Mignet, Considérant, Ward, Damer, Madame Marliani." Alexis de Tocqueville, the distinguished political writer who had discussed America with unusual perceptiveness for a Frenchman of his or any other epoch, was a Royalist and a supporter of the fallen regime; George Sand, who was repellent to him to begin with as a literary adventuress, had infuriated him by her articles supporting the Revolution; Considérant was a tub-thumping socialist who stood considerably to the left of George Sand, and as detestable to her as they both were to de Tocqueville. But rich as this combination was in its possibilities of discomfort, it was nothing in comparison with the presence in one room of George Sand, Prosper Mérimée, Count Alfred de Vigny, and Mme. Marliani. Mérimée had once spent a

night attempting, with diminishing enthusiasm, to overcome Sand's frigidity. She had gone the following day to
see her confidante, Marie Dorval, the actress who was de
Vigny's mistress, and had given her an account of the fiasco.
Marie Dorval had immediately communicated the grim
details to Dumas, another of her lovers; Dumas had evolved
a pithy phrase that reflected on Mérimée's virility and, having attributed it to George Sand herself, saw to it that it
was spread all over Paris. Mme. Marliani, the Italian wife
of the Spanish consul, was a notorious troublemaker and
mauvaise-langue who had a rather special relationship with
George Sand; she was intimate with her but not exactly
a friend. Her function was that of go-between in reverse;
when Sand had quarrelled with people and was no longer
on speaking terms with them but still wished to convey
something disagreeable and wounding to them, she would
put her venom in Mme. Marliani's mouth for delivery.
Mérimée preserved his calm throughout the evening in
Monckton Milnes' suite by affecting not to know who
George Sand was, and focussed his irritation on Mme.
Marliani, who responded by piling abuse upon all the
friends he had made on a recent visit to Spain. De Vigny
suffered, as he always did, in Sand's vicinity, possibly because he thought her a Lesbian and believed that she had
corrupted Marie Dorval; Sand relieved her feelings by talking politics at de Tocqueville, through Considérant's tirades.
She told him that, much as he disliked the moderate republican government, he would dislike the proletarian revolutionaries, whose success she predicted, even more. De
Tocqueville was fascinated by her forceful arguments and
by her; it was the first time an adherent from the enemy
political camp had ever spoken frankly to him, and he was

impressed. When, within the month, her predictions proved
to be altogether accurate, he was still more impressed, as
he tells us in his *Souvenirs*, in which this unusual dinner
and the June revolt in France figure as inseparable and
equally disagreeable experiences.

It is possible to recognize in these gatherings a Victorian
form of the brutal horseplay that was characteristic of
English society through the eighteenth century and the
Regency, and that went out of fashion as middle-class
hypocrisy took the place of aristocratic frankness as the
prevailing tone. It was entirely in keeping with this that
Monckton Milnes should have rounded out his practical
joke on the Archbishop of York with family prayers. It
was, indeed, his normal practice at Fryston to set an example to the lower orders in the village and on his estate
by regular churchgoing. But as a good host he did not com-
pel his visitors to go to church with him, and he provided
for their entertainment during his absence by showing
them where to find the choicer elements of his remarkable
collection of pornographic books and objects. This collection, Mr. Pope-Hennessy explains, was built up with
the aid of an individual called Fred Hankey, an English-
man whose career in Paris provides an admirable warning
against the dangers of taking people too seriously when
they are talking about themselves. Hankey met the Goncourt brothers in April of 1862 and knocked them into the
middle of the following week with a bravura performance.
Off they trotted to write it all down in the famous *Journal*:
"Today I visited a madman, a monster." There follows the
breathtaking description of the jaded, well-born, and degenerate English sadist which Professor Mario Praz has
shown, in his *The Romantic Agony*, to be one of the prin-

cipal sources of the great Latin-European myth about sadists. Alas, poor Fred Hankey was a vegetarian all his life because he could not bear the cruelty of butchering animals. He lived in apparently monogamous devotion to a French lady from whom he was inseparable, and after being cut off with a very small fortune by his father, a general, he made a living by acting as a purchasing agent for English collectors of Continental pornography. His Paris apartment, which the Goncourts took so seriously, was a showroom, and his talk was sales talk. The famous English collector Henry Spencer Ashbee, who was one of his most enthusiastic customers, tried to pretend in his own journal that meeting Hankey was an experience and that his agent was remarkable, but he was compelled to admit that Hankey struck him as "a de Sade *without the intellect*" and to note an expression "entirely devoid of energy or determination." The abominable abyss of vice, cruelty, and jaded sensationalism that the Goncourts saw behind Hankey was in fact the rather cozy little corner of the world in which Monckton Milnes and men like him spent the greater part of their time, energy, and money in evading boredom and the immense burden of thought.

Like poor Hankey, Monckton Milnes was always taken much more seriously abroad than at home. He was known to be a politician, and to be hand in glove with men like Lord Palmerston, the ebullient Prime Minister. When Monckton Milnes went to Europe in search of fresh gossip and new themes for practical jokes, we are informed by Mr. Pope-Hennessy, it was always assumed that he was on a secret mission, furthering the interests of perfidious Albion. It is true that he was a member of the House of Commons for a long time. But each speech he made was sillier

than the last, and each social occasion he attended showed
more clearly that he was a featherheaded rattle with neither
sense nor discretion, and his prospects rapidly declined.
He emitted, in public as in private, an overwhelming impression of futility, an impression so great that even though
Florence Nightingale was almost sure that she loved him,
she felt quite unable to marry him. His extraordinarily
naïve approach to Disraeli, whose contempt for him was
polite but profound, shows how far his unworldly silliness
could take him. When Disraeli wrote his political *roman
à clef* called *Coningsby*, which deals, among other things,
with the birth of the modern Conservative Party under his
own leadership, Milnes was devastated to find that he had
not been included as a character. He approached the author
to remonstrate with him, and said, almost weeping, that he
had often voted with Disraeli's Young England group and
that he deserved at least a mention. Disraeli obliged him
later by putting him into *Tancred* as Mr. Vavasour:

He liked to know everybody who was known, and to see
everything that ought to be seen. He also was of opinion that
everybody who was known ought to know him; and that the
spectacle, however splendid or exciting, was not quite perfect
without his presence. His life was a gyration of energetic
curiosity; an insatiable whirl of social celebrity. There was not
a congregation of sages or philosophers in any part of Europe
which he did not attend as a brother. He was present at the
camp of Kalisch in his yeomanry uniform, and assisted at the
festivals of Barcelona in an Andalusian jacket. He was everywhere and at everything; he had gone down in a diving bell
and gone up in a balloon.

In a private memorandum found among Disraeli's papers,
which Mr. Pope-Hennessy has been allowed to examine, the

exceedingly shrewd politician was more unkind. He had detected further shallows beneath Milnes' shallow surface. Milnes was ambitious, but he did not want any real power or responsibility. All he wanted was the fruit of success, for he did not wish to be successful in any line of endeavor. The crown he sought above everything else was elevation to the peerage—to be known as a lord, to become a nobleman. His relentless pursuit of this distinction makes him one of the great comic figures in English political and social history, and transforms the consistent mediocrity of his life and interests into a splendid comedy of the triumph of an almost absolute lack of merit. At the end of the long struggle, he realized that he was too grotesque a character to be given a title, and so set about getting one for his father, which he could inherit. His father, to his horror, refused the peerage Lord Palmerston offered by return of post. Milnes' agony at this reverse became so widely known and produced so much laughter that it actually created a wave of sympathy for the poor fellow, and after a time he was ennobled as Lord Houghton, out of Palmerston's warm-hearted kindness. The occasion was the marriage of Edward Prince of Wales to Alexandra of Denmark, and the peerage was handed out as part of the festivities. The *Daily Telegraph* found a graceful way of saying all that could possibly be said in favor of the new peer:

But it is not his politics that have earned Lord Houghton his enviable position—nor his poetry—nor his wealth, which is sufficient—nor his taste in art and literature, which is far above the average; but it is the combination of all these with the most extraordinary geniality.

He died in Vichy in 1885, at the age of seventy-six, in the middle of a religious argument carried on by letter with a friend who was an ardent Anglican churchman. A few days before he died he wrote:

I will not contradict anything you say except the *general usefulness* of suffering. I admit that it is so to the higher natures—but it is my decided experience that the mass of mankind are better for being happier. I am sure I am.

He died quite suddenly and unexpectedly, without any long preparatory illness, and one may imagine him, on the afternoon before his death, indulging in one of his favorite pastimes—totting up in one of the little reporter's notebooks he always had with him the names of all the distinguished, really distinguished, men and women he had shaken by the hand.

Lord Cardigan

The Reason Why, the latest of Mrs. Cecil Woodham-Smith's brilliant studies of life in Victorian England, takes its rather awkward title from one of Tennyson's worst and most popular poems. Tennyson's carpet-warrior streak had manifested itself as early as 1833 in his famous and ridiculous lines about Sir Galahad:

> My good blade carves the casques of men,
> My tough lance thrusteth sure,
> My strength is as the strength of ten,
> Because my heart is pure. . . .

> And when the tide of combat stands,
> Perfume and flowers fall in showers,
> That lightly rain from ladies' hands.

By 1854, when the Crimean War broke out, Tennyson had installed himself on the Isle of Wight, in Farringford, one of the most happily situated small houses in England, sheltered by dense thickets of pine, elm, holly, and laurel on land that was carpeted with wild flowers in spring, looking out over the quiet beauty of Freshwater Bay, and within a mile of the gleaming, peregrine-haunted white chalk cliff of High Down. On stormy nights, the wild music of the surf rolling in on the strand could be heard in the house, and on calm ones Tennyson often went out with the fishermen who worked off the beaches in open boats and set

their nets in the vast shadows of the cliff. It was a perfect
home and a perfect life for a romantic poet. Tennyson wan-
dered over the springy turf of the downs and through the
lanes by day and read enormously in the evenings. According to his wife's diary, he read aloud to her from Homer,
Virgil, Aeschylus, Euripides, Plato, the Bible, Molière,
Goethe, Dante, Theocritus, Catullus, Chaucer, Gray, Cole-
ridge, Shelley, Thackeray, and Hazlitt, and studied the
works of Spinoza, Berkeley, Kant, Schlegel, Fichte, Hegel,
and Ferrier. The fruit of all this was a passionate jingoism
and absorption in the Crimean War and a flaming hatred of
the peace party that had tried to keep England out of her
shoddy alliance with the Sultan of Turkey and Napoleon
III. On December 2, 1854, when the *Times* arrived with the
first account of the battle of Balaklava, Tennyson was in a
fit state of excitation to be inspired, and within a few minutes of reading it had churned out that enduring piece of
rubbish "The Charge of the Light Brigade." Its second
verse, from which the title of Mrs. Woodham-Smith's
biography of the Crimean War and some of its principal
figures derives, runs as follows:

> "Forward, the Light Brigade!"
> Was there a man dismay'd?
> Not tho' the soldier knew
> Someone had blunder'd.
> Theirs not to make reply,
> Theirs not to reason why,
> Theirs but to do and die.
> Into the valley of Death
> Rode the six hundred.

The rocking-horse heroics go on for another three verses
and then come to a conclusion:

When can their glory fade?
O the wild charge they made! . . .

Honor the Light Brigade,
Noble six hundred!

This gammon went straight to the hearts of the British people, and it became in time their equivalent of the ballad of "Barbara Frietchie."

The Light Brigade, led by Lord Cardigan, had indeed played an odd role in an unusual battle. The British Army in the Crimea had established its base at Balaklava, and had then set off on a march of two or three hours to besiege the Russian naval base of Sevastopol. Balaklava was surrounded by a sketchy defense line, three miles long, of small forts, guarded by eleven hundred Turkish troops, thirteen hundred British cavalrymen of the Light and Heavy Brigades, five hundred and fifty men of a Scotch regiment, and twelve hundred Marines. On October 24th, a Turkish spy brought in a fairly complete account of a Russian attack planned for the following day: twenty-five thousand Russians with thirty-eight guns were to move on the British base soon after dawn. Lord Raglan, the commander of the British forces, despised foreigners, and above all Turks, so his reaction to this report was to say, "Very well," and to take no action whatever. As a result, three fortifications in the center of the defense line, held by the eleven hundred Turks, were overrun by eleven thousand Russians in the early hours of the morning. By ten o'clock, the remaining Turks had had enough and were running down into Balaklava clamoring to be taken aboard ship. The eleven thousand Russians had broken through the defense line and, led by three or four thousand horsemen, were slowly bearing

down on the British base. There was nothing to stop them
but the Scotch regiment, the twelve hundred Marines, and
the two brigades of cavalry. At this moment, the Heavy
Brigade of five hundred men charged the three or four
thousand Russian cavalry in two waves. The first wave, led
by General James Scarlett, threw the Russians into disorder,
and the second wave broke them. The Russians began to
stream backward in rout. Scarlett's charge, uphill, and
against odds of six to one, is one of the great feats of arms
in military history, and it had a shattering effect on the
morale of the entire Russian force. The shock travelled
through it, and the attack ground to a standstill.

Lord Raglan and his staff had now reached a vantage
point where they could see the whole battlefield, and they
knew at once that it was a moment in which any action by
the British would have a decisive effect. Below them they
could see the Light Brigade drawn up in perfect order and
seemingly anchored to the ground. It had watched Scarlett's
charge. It had watched while Scarlett fought the Russians,
five hundred yards away, and now it watched as the Russians streamed off. Half an hour went by and the opportunity presented by the mob of flying Russian horsemen
was lost. Now Lord Raglan realized, because they had
brought up horse teams to haul away some captured guns,
that the shaken Russian infantry were getting ready to give
up the positions they had taken in the British defense line.
He sent down an order to the cavalry below him to attack
the Russians and prevent them from carrying off the guns.
The cavalry commander, Lord Lucan, a not especially intelligent man, did not understand the order. He took it to
apply to a body of Russians who were arrayed, with their
artillery, a mile up a valley both sides of which were in

Russian hands. Although it was inconceivable that cavalry would be asked to advance through a cross-fire to make a frontal attack on artillery batteries in position, Lord Lucan ordered the Light Brigade to do just this. Lord Cardigan boggled at the incredible order, then squared his shoulders and took the Brigade to destruction. As his squadrons trotted after him, an officer who had brought the order down through the chain of command from Lord Raglan, apparently recognizing that the troops were moving on the wrong objective, galloped diagonally across their front, pointing in the right direction. Lord Cardigan saw him but paid him no attention. Before the officer could do anything more, a bursting shell stripped open his side and bared his heart. Uttering an unearthly scream, the officer rode on across the front of the Light Brigade, rigid and still pointing in the right direction, until he fell dead from his saddle. The Brigade rode on over his body. Twenty minutes later defeat had been snatched from the jaws of victory. Five hundred and five of the seven hundred men in the Light Brigade were dead, and most of the hundred and ninety-five survivors were wounded. Five hundred of the horses were killed. The British Army was stunned, and the Russians withdrew with their captured guns unmolested. Lord Cardigan still was in a fury at the officer who had attempted to interfere with his attack order and who had screamed like a woman when he was hit. It was nothing to him that the Brigade was shattered; he had done his duty. Within a month, he completed the destruction of the Brigade by administrative inefficiency, leaving it encamped on high ground to face the full severity of the Russian winter and making no provision for feeding its horses. They starved or died of exposure. As there was nothing left to command,

Lord Cardigan obtained sick leave and went home, where, thanks to Tennyson's poem and the newspapers, he was received as a national hero.

Mrs. Woodham-Smith's fascinating study describes the ascent of this hero to his moment of greatness. He was an aristocrat and of noble blood, a member of the great family of Brudenell. The qualities that bring men to the top are not always obvious, and the ways blood will tell exercise theorists a good deal. There has been much talk lately of a finer sense of honor, of a deeper sense of social responsibility, and of an innate selflessness that mark the aristocrat from the bourgeois, particularly by the authors who are concerned with repudiating the corruptions of egalitarian liberalism. There is, luckily, very plain evidence of the special qualities that separated the Brudenells from the common run of men. The first Brudenell to acquire a title presented five thousand pounds in cash and a promissory note for a thousand pounds to the Duke of Buckingham, the King's favorite. Shortly after that, Charles I became aware of the unusual gifts that entitled Thomas Brudenell to the rank of baron. A further display of loyalty and devotion, in the form of a loan of a thousand pounds to Charles, secured the family an earldom. This family capacity for having large sums of cash on hand at the right moment was united with one for falling in love with young women of property, and by the time the hero was born the Cardigan estates ran to forty thousand acres and the Earl's income was the equivalent of a modern million dollars a year (after taxes). What effect being brought up as the heir to all this, and the only boy in a family of eight children, may have had on the Earl is uncertain, but he was thrown on his head by a horse when he was fourteen, and that had a considerable effect on his intellectual powers. When he was twenty-eight, he married a notoriously promiscuous lady, who was described by her first husband as the "most damned bad-tempered and extravagant bitch in the Kingdom," and when, at the age of twenty-seven, he entered the Army, he was known for his vile temper and as a bully who delighted in provoking duels. When he was thirty-five, he was allowed to purchase the command of the 15th Hussars. He instituted a remarkable system of getting secret reports on the officers under him from the sergeants and enlisted men, habitually lost his temper with his officers and insulted them in front of each other for not being so rich or well bred as he was, and persecuted those of them who, unlike him, had been on active service. After two years, he was removed from his command. This would have been the end of a mere mortal's Army career, but as this man was of noble stock he was again in command of a regiment, the 11th Light Dragoons, two years later. This time he rapidly made himself popular by having a man flogged on Easter Sunday, after the church parade, in the building in which the religious ceremony had taken place, and by attempting to murder an officer he disliked, Captain Harvey Tuckett, on a duelling ground. Captain Tuckett used the conventional smooth-bore duelling pistols of the time, but the Earl preferred to rely on French guns with rifled barrels. Cardigan shot Tuckett through the body, and when the news spread the enormous number of people who detested him eagerly waited to see him carried off to prison to do his time on the treadmill, which was what persons convicted of duelling could expect. But Cardigan belonged to that powerful trade union called the peerage, and rather than see justice done to a fellow-member, the peers were

prepared to swear their honor away. Cardigan was wangled
off the treadmill by one of the most ignoble legal quibbles
that have ever disfigured a court of law. He had been ar-
rested with a smoking pistol in his hand while Tuckett was
lying on the ground before him. But who was Tuckett?
He was known to everyone as Captain Harvey Tuckett,
but the defense argued:

> The prosecutor is bound to prove the Christian and surnames
> of the person against whom the offence is alleged; if he fails
> in either, he fails in the proof of his case. Every count in the
> indictment contains the name of Harvey Garnett Phipps
> Tuckett. There is no evidence to show that the person at whom
> the noble lord shot upon the 12th September was Harvey Gar-
> nett Phipps Tuckett . . . there is nothing to connect this Mr.
> Tuckett with the person who is said to have been on Wim-
> bledon Common on the 12th September.

The Chief Justice, Lord Denman, agreed; everyone concerned knew that Captain Harvey Tuckett had been on
Wimbledon Common on the morning of the duel, none of
them knew that Captain Harvey Garnett Phipps Tuckett
had been there. The solemn farce then proceeded with the
Chief Justice asking each peer in turn, "How says your
lordship, is James Thomas Earl of Cardigan guilty of the
felony of which he stands indicted, or not guilty?" And
all but one of the peers of England, with their hands on
their hearts, answered, "Not guilty, upon my honor."

The next phase of Lord Cardigan's life was largely occupied with nonmilitary matters. There was an exceedingly
public scandal about his adultery with Lady Frances Paget,
and another when his wife left him for Lord Colville. Cardigan took to spending less and less time with his regiment
and more and more in Paris and on board his splendid yacht,

the *Dryad*, in the ambiguous company of a Mr. Hubert de Burgh. Mrs. Woodham-Smith politely remarks that he frequently acted on the Earl's behalf "in negotiations of delicacy." He seems to have been a kind of pander.

When the Crimean War broke out, the Earl of Cardigan, now fifty-seven, was aging rapidly, suffering from chronic bronchitis, and under treatment for an irritating bladder complaint. The British cavalry at that time was well officered by men in their thirties who had learned their trade in hard fighting against the Marathas and the Sikhs in India. It was only natural that when a general for the Light Brigade should be looked for these men should be passed over and the Earl of Cardigan should be appointed. It was as natural to appoint Lord Lucan commander of the cavalry division and Lord Cardigan's immediate superior. Lucan's temper was worse than Cardigan's, and he had not been in command of troops for seventeen years. He was fifty-four, he had been on notoriously bad terms with Cardigan for a considerable time, and it was widely believed that only the intervention of the Duke of Wellington had prevented them from fighting a duel. From the moment of their appointment, every officer in the Army knew that disaster impended. The disaster was the destruction of the Light Brigade. Whether Mrs. Woodham-Smith intended it to be so or not, the fascinating background story of the death in action of this splendid fighting unit is a forceful indictment of aristocracy and the aristocratic principle.

Perhaps the most interesting section of the book describes the pathetic self-liquidation of Lord Cardigan as a national hero. His bombast, his insatiable appetite for greater recognition, his determination to keep old feuds going, in the end destroyed him in a fire of pitiless publicity. Tennyson came to see that he had blundered and that his "perfume and flowers" had been delivered at the wrong address. He talked the whole thing over in 1881 with his friend Brigadier General Sir Edward Hamley, the author of *Operations of War*, and with Alexander Kinglake, the author of *The Invasion of the Crimea*. They persuaded him that it had not been the Earl of Cardigan at Balaklava, not at all; it had been Scarlett's day. So the rocking horse was mounted once again and a new poem was dutifully produced, this time called "The Charge of the Heavy Brigade":

> For our men gallopt up with a cheer and a shout
> And the foeman surged, and waver'd, and reel'd
> Up the hill, up the hill, up the hill, out of the field
> And over the brow and away.
> Glory to each and to all, and the charge that they made!
> Glory to all the three hundred, and all the Brigade!

But the times had changed. By now the American Civil War had been fought; the world had heard the contemptuous Confederates shouting, as the Federal cavalry lined up to charge, "Here come those damn fools with their sabres!" And the newer, nastier battlefields were dominated by the ugly, tearing sound of the first machine guns firing their bursts. When two emissaries from America brought one of Mr. Edison's astonishing new machines to Farringford to record Tennyson's voice, he was able to roar "The Charge of the Heavy Brigade" into the speaking tube "in a voice of amazing power," but it was too late to get the message through. The age of Galahad, glittering and jingling on horseback, had gone for good.

Darwin and Huxley

Apes, Angels, and Victorians, a study of the lives and work of Charles Darwin and Thomas Huxley by Professor William Irvine, of Stanford University, is an admirable example of what is known in academic circles as "well-documented biography." This, as opposed to the "conversational (and therefore, from an academic point of view, worthless) biography of the Lytton Strachey and David Cecil schools, wears its research on its sleeve in the form of little numbers [173] which spot the text like currants in a bun, and thus demonstrates its fundamental seriousness and freedom from literary vice. Professor Irvine provides a fine example of the documentation method on page 11, where he is dealing with an incident in the early life of Huxley (Huxley was sixteen years younger than Darwin, so, of course, his early years are described first):

At thirteen or fourteen, he had suffered a more lurid illumination. Two of his elder sisters had married physicians, and he had been thrown a good deal with medical students. Having through his reading acquired a knowledge of the human body, he went with some of his new friends to a post-mortem examination, which probably took place in a typical close, dark, village dissecting room of the period. Mr. Houston Peterson re-creates the scene:

"He suddenly finds himself in the presence of a naked human corpse. He is almost stifled by the mortuary & medicinal

96

odors. He shudders inwardly as he sees the first large incision made in the torso. He sees exposed the lungs and heart, the stomach and bowels. The knives work quickly, cruelly. The dissectors are casual and matter-of-fact about their business. Now a serious remark, now a little joke. And young Huxley stands there, not for a few minutes—but for two or three hours, gratifying his scientific and morbid curiosity." [5]

Immediately afterward he sank into "a strange state of apathy," which seemed so serious that his father sent him away to friends in Warwickshire. There he soon recovered, but for the rest of his life suffered from "internal pain" and "hypochondriacal dyspepsia." Though he had exhibited no physical symptoms, he always believed that he had been "poisoned somehow." No doubt he had suffered a severe mental shock. Still believing in God and immortality, he had suddenly been confronted, at the sensitive period of adolescence, with a bloody and nauseating spectacle of physical death. Apparently, he had identified himself with the corpse. Recovery was a return to life.

"I remember staggering from my bed to the window on the bright spring morning after my arrival, and throwing open the casement. Life seemed to come back on the wings of the breeze, and to this day the faint odour of woodsmoke, like that which floated across the farm yard in the early morning, is as good to me as the 'sweet south upon a bed of violets.' " [6]

Mr. Peterson maintains that as Huxley's later outbursts of temper and virtuous indignation were probably produced by the nervous strain of a strenuous sense of duty, so his aggressiveness was the result of a fear neurosis springing from his early encouter with a human corpse.

This passage can profitably be compared with a quotation from Thomas Huxley's biographical sketch of himself in the two-volume American edition of Leonard Huxley's life and letters of his father:

As I grew older, my great desire was to be a mechanical engineer, but the fates were against this, and while very young I commenced the study of medicine under a medical brother-in-law. But, though the Institute of Mechanical Engineers would certainly not own me, I am not sure that I have not all along been a sort of mechanical engineer *in partibus infidelium.* I am now occasionally horrified to think how little I ever knew or cared about medicine as the art of healing. The only part of my professional course which really and deeply interested me was physiology, which is the mechanical engineering of living machines; and, notwithstanding that natural science has been my proper business, I am afraid there is very little of the genuine naturalist in me. I never collected anything, and species work was always a burden to me; what I cared for was the architectural and engineering part of the business, the working out of the wonderful unity of plan in the thousands and thousands of diverse living constructions, and the modifications of similar apparatuses to serve diverse ends. The extraordinary attraction I felt towards the study of the intricacies of living structures nearly proved fatal to me at the outset. I was a mere boy—I think between thirteen and fourteen years of age— when I was taken by some older student friends of mine to the first post-mortem examination I ever attended. All my life I have been most unfortunately sensitive to the disagreeables which attend anatomical pursuits, but on this occasion my curiosity overpowered all other feelings, and I spent two or three hours in gratifying it. I did not cut myself, and none of the ordinary symptoms of dissection-poison supervened, but poisoned I was somehow, and I remember sinking into a strange state of apathy. By way of a last chance, I was sent to the care of some good kind people, friends of my father's, who lived in a farmhouse in the heart of Warwickshire.

The "woodsmoke" lines quoted by Professor Irvine follow, and are immediately succeeded by this sentence:

I soon recovered, but for years I suffered from occasional paroxysms of internal pain, and from that time my constant friend, hypochondriacal dyspepsia, commenced his half century of co-tenancy of my fleshly tabernacle.

The Irvine passage reads as if it were a loose rewrite of the Leonard Huxley passage, and the authority quoted seems merely to have jazzed up the account of the post-mortem and fattened it until it could support the airy-fairy speculation about a "fear neurosis." The passage simply omits Huxley's explicitly expressed awareness of the relation between the event and his later ill-health, as well as the revealing statement of his mechanistic approach to biology—a statement that is fundamental to an understanding of his career as a scientist. Professor Irvine, though he does not quote the statement, does not disregard it, either, for presently he uses it as the basis for a remarkable theory about Huxley's character, which he advances to explain why, in spite of a great admiration for Carlyle, Huxley did not become a literary man:

Huxley was too little attracted to the characteristic subject matter of the writer. He became interested in man as a physical mechanism, as an anthropoid ape, as a social unit and a citizen, as a delicate machine for the discovery of scientific truth, but never to any appreciable extent in man as a personality and a human being. With all his splendid talents for friendship and affection, he remained, from the psychological point of view, largely indifferent to people.

This would be all very well if there were not plentiful evidence to the contrary. For example, Dr. Anton Dohrn, the founder of the Marine Biological Station in Naples, was received as a stranger into the Huxley family while they were summering at Swanage in 1867, and went away a life-long friend, writing soon afterward to a German acquaintance:

I have been reading several chapters of Mill's *Utilitarianism* today, and met with the word "happiness" more than once; if *I* had to give anybody a definition of this much debated word I should say—go and see the Huxley family at Swanage; and if you would enjoy the same I enjoyed, you would feel what is happiness, and never more ask for a definition of this sentiment.

Leonard Huxley quotes this letter and one written about his father by Leslie Stephen, the father of Virginia Woolf. It is admittedly a letter of condolence, but Stephen was not given to insincerities:

But what now dwells most in my mind is the memory of old kindness, and of the days when I used to see him with you and his children. I may safely say that I never came from your house without thinking how good he is; what a tender and affectionate nature the man has!

Professor Irvine does not explain how indifference to people, even of a kind visible only from a psychological point of view, could create such impressions of warmth and receptiveness.

After Huxley has been invested with his "fear neurosis," Irvine goes on to Darwin and the problems of his ill-health:

Dr. Douglas Hubble is convinced he was shamming, or at least he regards the illness as psychopathic, having its cause in environmental factors and, by a pleasant irony, chiefly in the puzzled paternal physician himself. Dr. Robert Darwin's cold and gloomy tyranny had resulted in a household of "disagreeable and unfulfilled daughters and neurotic sons." [34] His elder son Erasmus was so lamed in initiative that he was capable of nothing but graceful bachelordom, and Charles was left with a morbid craving for affection that encouraged excessive care from his wife and so led to lifelong hypochondriacal illness.

Note [34] does not, as one would expect, refer to any proof that the daughters were disagreeable or the sons neurotic, but simply takes one back to where Dr. Hubble made his assertion. The fact is that Charles Darwin emerged from this temple of cold and gloomy tyranny with the impression that his father was "the kindest man I ever knew," and that while making a contribution to the science of his time equalled in the extent of its effects only by Newton's *Principia*, he married and gave his many children a magnificent start in life in a tranquil and consistently happy home. To describe this professionally and personally creative life as neurotic is odd, but Professor Irvine goes further than that:

Dr. Hubble concedes that Darwin's illness may also have had some hereditary basis. In another illuminating diagnosis, Dr. Walter C. Alvarez stresses this factor, describing Darwin as an asthenic or "constitutional inadequate." [37] Nervous tension frequently expresses itself in visceral disturbances and may be due, according to Dr. Alvarez, to a neural weakness closely related to insanity.

Again, number [37] refers one not to a source that discloses constitutional weaknesses in Charles Darwin's make-up but to a work in which Dr. Alvarez made his guess about Darwin sixty-one years after his subject's death. Darwin could shoot twenty-three snipe with twenty-four shots, and often killed wild birds and animals by throwing a geologist's hammer at them. This argues unusually good muscular coördination and better than average condition, while his performances show the initial strength of his constitution.

When he was attached to the expedition which, on board H.M.S. *Beagle*, was surveying the southern coast of South America, he spent the best part of five years in the icy and stormy waters off Cape Horn and the Falkland Islands. On his shore trips he rode horseback, sometimes spending ten hours at a stretch in the saddle, on journeys of up to five hundred miles. He went along on the expedition's ascent of the Santa Cruz River, in Argentina, taking his turn on the towlines with which the ship's boats were hauled upstream for over a hundred miles against the seven-knot current, and sleeping at night in the open on the frozen ground beside a campfire. He climbed a twelve-thousand-foot peak in the Andes, and did many other things that demonstrated better than average physical powers. The food on the *Beagle* was amazingly poor; when the ship picked up five deserters from a New Bedford whaler who had been living in the open on Chiloé Island, off the South American coast, for fourteen months, it was remarked that they were in better shape than most members of the *Beagle*'s crew. The account of the expedition by the captain of the *Beagle* says that several of his men died during the voyage. It seems not unlikely that five years of undernourishment in cramped and insanitary quarters left their mark on Darwin, as naval service in similar conditions marked many other men. At any rate, his exposure to hardship during the *Beagle* expedition is a matter of fact, while the Hubble-bubble about his neuroses is a matter of conjecture that is, at this distance in time from the living mind, simply not worth making. Or rather, it is worth making only because the tactic of presenting rationalist leaders as neurotics is in keeping with the tenets of the anti-rational and anti-intellectual obscurantist movement that now is gaining so much ground.

The extent to which this turn of thought appears to have affected this new study of Darwin and Huxley becomes evident when the mature years of the two men are under consideration. After Darwin returned from the *Beagle* expedition, he suffered the humiliation of being compelled to farm out his zoological specimens to other men for classification, because he did not have the groundwork in natural science that would enable him to do this work himself. Had he advanced the theory of evolution any earlier than he did, he would undoubtedly have been dismissed for the same reason that Lamarck was—on the basis that he was a speculative litterateur whose guesses couldn't be taken seriously. Darwin was extremely conscious of this situation, for there was such a litterateur in his own family—Erasmus Darwin, his grandfather, who had made a great many hypotheses (and himself) ridiculous by advancing them as intuitions unsupported by any evidence or observation. Charles had, moreover, studied under Six Alexander Grant, a Lamarckian, in Edinburgh. Dr. Grant, his instructor in marine zoology, provided him with a lesson in the value of evidence. He informed Darwin with authority that he knew that certain vesicles found in tidal pools on the seashore were seeds of a locally plentiful rockweed. Darwin, who was then just seventeen, presently made the discovery that some of the vesicles were in fact the young of a kind of leech and that the others were members of a hitherto unobserved genus. Professor Irvine, who passes over Darwin's serious work with Grant in silence, treats his eminently reasonable desire to support his hypotheses with conclusive evidence as a neurotic trait:

One is tempted to see in these qualities further evidence of the effect of his father on him—in the dogged patience, a passionate desire to win respect and love; in the reluctance to speculate and the eagerness to return again and again to the facts for corroboration, a sence of insecurity born of many shattering explosions of paternal wrath.

For anyone who holds these views, it is easy to take a patronizing line about the length of time Darwin spent studying barnacles. "And there were odd facts, satisfying to a man with an appetite for odd facts. . . . But were even such facts worth eight years?" Professor Irvine points out that Bulwer-Lytton apparently modelled an over-zealous fictional professor on Darwin, and then an informed comment by Huxley is introduced, though attached to an insulating phrase of denigration: "With characteristic enthusiasm for feats of scientific industry, Huxley agreed" (that the facts *were* worth while). Irvine comes at last to the real point, contained in Sir Joseph Hooker's remark that Darwin was "a trained naturalist after, and only after," the barnacles.

Another point of the greatest interest is, however, passed over in silence. Anti-Darwinians are fond of pretending there is a characteristically nineteenth-century flavor to the evolutionary theory that the phrase "the survival of the fittest" is a concept flattering to mankind generally and to the prosperous middle class in particular—the implication being that Darwin, a member of the prosperous middle class, cooked up the theory to prove that the entire historical process had worked to produce the social order in which that class was preëminent. Equally grotesque is the pretense that Darwin was putting forth the idea that evolution is a sort of beneficent goddess conducting all species along a path of inevitable betterment, with occasional "exams" leading to a kind but firm extinction of failures and to prizes for the successful. One of Darwin's observations on barnacles runs as follows:

I can hardly express the perplexity which I felt when I first examined Proteolepas, and when I naturally mistook the mouth for the entire head, for I saw, as I thought, the antennae in direct connection with the second segment of the body! It was quite as monstrous and incredible an inversion of the laws of nature as those fabulous half-human monsters, with an eye seated in the middle of their stomachs. . . . I fully believe that we here see an articulate animal in which the whole of the three anterior segments of the head have been, during the act of metamorphosis, absolutely aborted, with the exception of a mere rudiment on the ventral surface . . . developed as a covering for the two cement-ducts.

What is being described is a process of functional adaptation in which a considerable part of an animal's head has been reduced to a mere protective shell. This Darwinian observation of regression is fatal to the pretense that he believed in inevitable betterment. It may be that the patient work that led him to purge *The Origin of Species* of the inevitable-betterment idea, an idea the obscurantists love to call "the liberal fallacy," was inspired by the "sense of insecurity" Professor Irvine dotes upon, but it seems much more likely that Darwin simply embarked on a line of research to test a hypothesis and carried it through until a conclusion could legitimately be drawn.

Irvine's denigration of Huxley, which follows a similar pattern, includes the remark that "as a scientist, he favored more government because he favored more sanitation, research, education, more scientific posts for scientific men." This attribution of motive again blithely ignores certain facts. During Huxley's lifetime, Britain transformed itself from a primarily agricultural country into an industrial one, and in doing so more than doubled its population. More government was wanted for the common-sense reason that there was more to govern. There was a sound sociological reason for persuading government to enlarge itself by assuming the function of an educator, a reason that has nothing to do with a belief in more government for its own sake. The new urban proletariat created by industrialism was breeding at a rate that would soon make it a dominant mass in society, and it was brutalized by poverty of a kind almost unimaginable by modern Westerners to a point at which its members seemed to belong to a race utterly different from the well-to-do. If this savage mass had continued to develop as it had done between 1800 and 1850, it would certainly have frustrated the construction of an orderly society. Huxley believed in state education, as all liberals do, not because there is any virtue in state control as such but because he felt that an uneducated proletariat is social nitroglycerine, an unstable jelly that any shock can touch off, and he preferred civilization to anarchy. It was this preference, and not any fear neurosis or sense of insecurity, that produced Huxley's passion for controversy with churchmen and politicians. For him, a morality or social ethos based on revealed religion was fundamentally unsound, because sooner or later it took one back to a universe in which the mind of a creator was the focal point. This concept leads to all kinds of anthropomorphic introductions of purpose and design into the working of natural forces, and in the end to a picture of a rational universe governed by law. Scientific method produces no evidence that will support this picture, and a great deal that is fatal to it. Huxley thought that a schizoid society drawing its morality and values from a compartment of its collective mind where faith preserved a revealed truth which scientific method demolished in another compartment was in for serious trouble. It would be better for mankind to abandon revealed truth as a basis for action and to proceed on the basis of what is ascertainable; a true morality and a system of values could be based on a dispassionate examination of man's relation with man. With this in mind, Huxley declared his controversial purposes:

We shall never think rightly in politics until we have cleared our minds of delusions, and more especially of the philosophical delusions, which, as I have endeavoured to show, have infested political thought for centuries. . . . Ground must be cleared and levelled before a building can be properly commenced; the labour of the navvy is as necessary as that of the architect, however much less honored; and it has been my humble endeavour to grub up those old stumps of the *a priori* which stand in the way of the very foundations of a sane political philosophy. To those who think that questions of the kind I have been discussing have merely an academic interest, let me suggest once more that a century ago Robespierre and St. Just proved that the way of answering them may have extremely practical consequences.

It is possible to criticize the inconsistencies in Huxley's metaphysics, but the fortunes of the schizoid society in the present century provide reason for suspecting that the rational approach to human affairs that he based on Darwin's picture of the human place in the universe may be the only one that offers mankind any hope of happiness at all.

Charles Dickens

Mr. Edgar Johnson's critical Book-of-the-Month Club biography, *Charles Dickens*, is at once an admirable account of the great entertainer's day-to-day life and a pious absurdity that rates him above Dostoevski and alongside Shakespeare and Balzac as one of the creative geniuses of all literature. It would be just as absurd to deny that he was a genius of this order, and yet, for all his abundance of invention, vitality of expression, and richness of imagination, he cannot keep such company for even a moment. Mr. Johnson asserts that he can, but there are the books themselves, and they, alas, are hostile witnesses. The situation of Lady Dedlock in *Bleak House* is one that Balzac might have devised, and the emotional tension of the scene in which the great lady is told by the dingy, pushing solicitor's clerk that he has grubbed up all the details of the scandal that will ruin her is fully worthy of him. But as the scene draws to its end the lights go down, the realistic set vanishes, Lady Dedlock advances to center stage bathed in a spotlight and, clasping her hands on her bosom, addresses the back row of the gallery:

"O my child, my child! Not dead in the first hours of her life, as my cruel sister told me; but sternly nurtured by her, after she had renounced me and my name! O my child, O my child!"

108

It is the same barnstormer's language that Louisa Grad-grind speaks in *Hard Times*, when she has to tell her father what an awful wrong he did her by selling her to a rich husband:

"How could you give me life, and take from me all the in-appreciable things that raise it from the state of conscious death? Where are the graces of my soul? Where are the senti-ments of my heart? What have you done, O father, what have you done, with the garden that should have bloomed once, in this great wilderness here?"
She struck herself with both her hands upon her bosom.

Here, too, there is another Balzacian situation; the girl has a husband she does not love, she has seen her brother turned into a gambler and toady to well-to-do men as a result of her marriage, she is being seduced by a cold and calculating man who knows just how to exploit her un-happiness, and she is being spied on by unfriendly servants. But when a lady strikes her bosom and speaks of gardens that should have bloomed within it one cannot either be-lieve her or believe in her. Like G. K. Chesterton, Mr. Johnson defends this falsity resolutely, particularly in *The Old Curiosity Shop*, where it crops up at its worst. The fault, according to him, is not Dickens; the fault is in the modern reader, who is made ashamed by honest expressions of natural sentiment and can be bribed into being moved by death scenes and the like only if they are legitimized by complex ideas about the problem of evil and pain. It is for this reason that the modern reader can let himself go over the death of Ilusha in *The Brothers Karamazov* but flinches from a healthy reaction to the death of Little Nell. Yet it is not, as Chesterton pretended, the thought of the death of a lovable child from which the critical reader shrinks; it is the Dickensian device of extracting an emotional dividend from the death:

When Death strikes down the innocent and young, for every fragile form from which he lets the panting spirit free, a hundred virtues rise, in shapes of mercy, charity, and love, to walk the world, and bless it. Of every tear that sorrowing mortals shed on such green graves, some good is born, some gentler nature comes.

Mr. Johnson seems perverse rather than bold when he says that "It is in fact not we, but Dickens and the Victorians, who are in the central stream of natural emotion," for it does not really appear either natural or pleasant to pretend that the loss of happiness and delight involved in a child's death brings a gain of any kind.

The thing that keeps Dickens out of the company to which Mr. Johnson would elevate him is clearest in the history of *The Old Curiosity Shop*, of which Mr. Johnson tells only a part. Little Nell began life as a character in a short story that was to have been published in the third number of a weekly miscellany, written entirely by Dickens, called *Master Humphrey's Clock*. The first number was an enormous success, because the public took it to be a new novel, and the second a failure. When he saw that people did not want to buy unrelated short stories, he hauled *The Old Curiosity Shop* out of the third number and announced that it would appear in the fourth as the first chapter of a serial. He then settled down to force this novel out, week by week, with no definite idea of where he was heading except that it was toward a happy ending. But when his friend John Forster, whose insen-

sitivity and pretentiousness later on gave Dickens the character of Podsnap, wrote to him suggesting that it would
be a wonderful idea to kill his heroine off so that her
girlish charm would never be touched by maturity or age,
he fell in love with the notion. It made him think with
the liveliest emotion of his wife's sister, Mary Hogarth,
who had died when she was seventeen and had thus escaped
the changes that five pregnancies and an anemic disorder
had by then inflicted on Catherine Dickens. As soon as
Nell was doomed it was an easy matter for him to discover
what the book was to be about:

When I first began [he wrote to Forster] on your valued
suggestion, to keep my thoughts upon this ending of the tale, I
resolved to try and do something which might be read by
people about whom Death had been, with a softened feeling,
and with consolation.

The intention is kindly, but it is not an artist's intention.
There is no doubt that Dickens now saw exactly what he
was doing and knew the difference between one intention
and the other, A few years after he had written *The
Old Curiosity Shop*, he began a book that was planned
around the superbly conceived character of Mr. Pecksniff
(founded, according to a recent biography by Mr. John
Summerson, on the architect Nash) as an attack on hypocrisy. It was to have opened with a stage direction designed
to startle the reader: "Your homes the scenes, yourselves
the actors, here!" But this was removed before publication,
for fear of unfavorable public reaction, and when sales of
the weekly parts proved that the attack on hypocrisy was
too close to home for most readers, Pecksniff was broad-
ened into a figure of farce and Martin Chuzzlewit was sent

off to America, out of the danger area. The sales were still disappointing, so Mrs. Gamp was invented, as proof that the thing was pantomime and not satire and that no offense was intended. The Balzacian comedy of greed and humbug that is discernible in the early chapter in which the pack of legacy-hunting relatives close in around the sickbed of the misanthropic elder Chuzzlewit was dropped in favor of a charade in which the misanthrope turned out to have a heart of gold and virtue triumphed by hitting vice with a slapstick. It is not that Dickens lacked control of his material; he had complete command of it, but his acute sensitivity to public response overrode all aesthetic necessity and he was prepared to break step and change direction at any time. When he started to write *Dombey and Son,* an important ingredient of the story was to be the moral breakup of Walter Gay. But Forster-Podsnap declared that the public would not stand for the conversion of a nice young man into a nasty one. So the story merely tells how Mr. Dombey became a dear old gentleman. It is not too much to say that in this book a great artist gave up his birthright once and for all and became an entertainer.

Mr. Johnson will have none of this; for him Dickens matures as a social critic and a dauntless radical with *Dombey and Son.* It appears that his development along this line began with *A Christmas Carol.*

Scrooge has lost his way between youth and maturity. Society too in the course of its development has gone astray and then hardened itself in obdurate error with a heartless economic theory. Scrooge's conversion is more than the transformation of a single human being. It is a plea for society itself to undergo a change of heart. . . . When Scrooge has truly changed, and has dispatched the anonymous gift of the turkey to Bob Cratchit as an earnest of repentance, he may go to his nephew's house and ask wistfully, "Will you let me in, Fred?" With love reanimated in his heart, he may hope for love.

Mr. Johnson proceeds to say that "It may be that what really gives the skeptics pause is that Scrooge is converted to a gospel of good cheer. They could probably believe easily enough if he espoused some gloomy doctrine of intolerance." Perhaps, but the real objection is that love is awfully cheap at the price of a turkey and a little snivelling. And since Scrooge is like no one who ever was, the attack on heartless economic theory is a safety play that can be relied upon to ruffle nobody.

The strong point in Mr. Johnson's case for Dickens as a fearless social critic is *Hard Times*, a novel Macaulay referred to as "sullen socialism" and that Shaw made much of when claiming its author as a Socialist propagandist. But the point is not as strong as it looks. In *Hard Times*, Dickens toiled along a path clearly marked out by Mrs. Gaskell and Disraeli in their attacks on the brutalities of industrialism, and what set him at it was a wave of demand for reform aroused by the scathing reports of various Parliamentary committees of inquiry. In pitching into the manufacturers, Dickens was showing all the courage of a man who falls in at the rear of a victory parade. He exploited the reformist mood and produced a best-seller; he was, as usual, following his public. The book is, moreover, dubious social criticism, and one can only suppose that when Shaw wrote about it he was confident that his audience would remember his own exposition and forget Dickens. At all events, he had the nerve to object to the union leader in the book as a caricature and its one blemish. The representative of the manufacturers, to whom Shaw raised no objection, is a Mr. Bounderby, who pretends, as so many industrialists do, that he was abandoned by his mother in infancy and left in the care of a drunken grandmother. His mother, who was really a respectable village shopkeeper, gave him a very fair start in life. Bounderby repays her for this by allowing her thirty pounds a year, on condition that she never come near him, a promise she breaks by coming once a year in disguise to peep at her dear, ungrateful boy. The book is as childish in its ignorance of what businessmen are like or were like as it is in its conception of industrial problems.

Dickens' imagination, in matters of finance, never got beyond petty cash. None of his rich men are really wealthy, and none of them are engaged in credible affairs. *Hard Times* is, however, wholehearted in its attack on two things —education and Parliament—that were the really effective instruments of social reform, and its only positive doctrine is that circus people are wiser and kinder than schoolmasters and politicians. In the face of the brutal conflicts of a primitive industrial society, Dickens' gospel of good cheer shows up poorly. As if thoroughly aware of the fact, he made no further attempt to grapple with realism but retired into the strange, Gothic magnificence of his fantasy world of vanished wills, veiled women searching for their lost pasts, men living under false names, and wronged children. To Taine's lucid French mind it seemed that in his later books Dickens was treading on the edge of lunacy because of his obsession with darkness and violence, but Mr. Johnson, in line with much recent criticism, sees him following a course of development along sound Marxist lines. The theory produces comic effects that are, it is to be feared, unintentional. In

Great Expectations, Pip and Estella are undone not by simple pride and snobbery but by the corrupt values of bourgeois society; this in some way makes them seem like Adam and Eve and leads to a quotation from Milton. Mr. Johnson does even better things with *Edwin Drood,* in which the wicked Jasper smokes opium in a dive frequented by Chinese and Lascars and Drood says he means to go to Egypt:

It is not only the London docks and slums, the smoke-blackened cities of the north, that are strangled in its coils, but India, Egypt, China, the victims of the opium trade, subject peoples, everywhere, falling prey to a greedy Imperialism.

Young Drood mouths the catchwords of that Imperialism in their most infuriating form. He is "Going to wake up Egypt a little," he says patronizingly. Like any acquisitive materialist, he is condescending about the life of reflective thought. "Reading?" he asks with a trace of contempt. . . . He talks with insolent and insular contempt of other races. . . . His words briefly epitomize the whole vainglorious gospel of backward races and the white man's mission.

Instead, therefore, of abandoning the analysis of society, Dickens has deepened it, for he has sensed the extension of the struggle to take in the entire world. Despite its somnolent air of peace, behind Cloisterham lurk all those inhumanities he has spent his life in fighting, grown more monstrous than ever as they threaten now a dark resentful conflict of East and West.

This bizarre presentation of Dickens as an anti-imperialist in the mood of the nineteen-twenties looks more than a little absurd. It has to be compared with an outburst called forth by the Indian Mutiny which Mr. Johnson has published elsewhere, in his edition of Dickens' letters to Miss Angela Burdett-Coutts (*The Heart of Charles Dickens*).

This declares, in rather less acceptable terms, his real feelings about the lesser breeds without the law:

And I wish I were Commander in Chief in India. The first thing I would do . . . should be to proclaim to them, in their language, that . . . I should do my utmost to exterminate the Race upon whom the stain of the late cruelties rested . . . that I was there for that purpose and no other, and was now proceeding, with all convenient dispatch and merciful swiftness of execution, to blot it out of mankind and raze it off the face of the Earth.

My love to Mrs. Brown . . .

The gospel of good cheer, it would seem, was either not for export or lacked the strength to stand up to shocks. A considerable number of these letters deal with Dickens' interventions in the management of a home for fallen women financed by Miss Burdett-Coutts, and they reinforce one's doubts about both the gospel and his grasp of realities. The girls were mostly illiterate or nearly so, ragged and desperate delinquent children.

In their living room I have put up two little inscriptions selected from the sermons of Jeremy Taylor and Barrow . . . also a little inscription of my own, referring to the advantages of order, punctuality, and good temper.

They were elaborately teased by a fiendish device called Captain Maconochie's Mark System:

I propose to limit the reward for "Voluntary Self Denial," to abstinence from beer, on the part of those employed in the laundry on Washing-days . . . and to abstinence on other days from tea and sugar. . . . It is not unlikely that some young woman may now and then deny herself her beer or tea because she is sulky. In that case, I would either not mark it as "Voluntary Self Denial" at all, or would mark it at the reduced amount of 2.

Occasionally the accent of Pecksniff himself is detectable: "The two best things I observed in her were, her trembling very much while I was talking to her, and her being extremely grateful when I gave her hope." And sometimes the voice is uglier, as when Dickens, having given an unruly girl to understand that she was going to be put out on the street in the rags in which she was admitted to the home, has her sent to jail for two months "of Mr. Tracey's severest discipline" for stealing some clothes and escaping ahead of the time set for her expulsion.

These letters show Dickens oddly at a loss outside the world of his imagination. Mr. Johnson's biography supports this feeling that he was in a complex way disabled from making contact with realities. His relations with his publishers, with lawyers, and with his afflicted wife all show that he was utterly incapable of recognizing the obligations and rapports of normal business and social life. When he wished to change publishers it was never because of a simple matter of business; it was always because he had been betrayed or wronged. And when he wished to leave his wife after falling in love with a young actress it was not because of his own emotional instability; the breakup of the marriage was due entirely to his wife's defects. It had to be. He appears to have really believed in that melodramatic world of wholly evil schemers and wholly good good people with whom his books nearly always deal. The evil people tried to frustrate him, the good fell in with his plans, and since he generally got his way the happy ending came to seem almost inevitable. But not quite; he never outgrew his fear of the terrible five months during which his father went to debtors' prison and he had to go into a factory like a common workingman. He could never he sure that he had not lost his status as a gentleman. This cut him off from easy intercourse with his intellectual equals all through his life and made him surround himself with an entourage of second-raters. It accounts, too, for the obsessive hunger for the reassurance of popularity and applause, which eventually turned him into an actor. The terrors and nightmares that affected Taine so disagreeably are all concerned with loss of status, and the clamor for social reform is in reality an attack on the inhabitants of social levels at which he felt unsure of himself. The attack sharpens as he grows more successful, but his success fails to establish his social rank with any certainty. The only area in which Dickens' gift could serenely release itself was the one he could recognize as being below him and no source of challenge, that of the poor relation, the tradesman, the artisan, and the bohemian. Below that lay another world of pure terror, the world of the really poor, in which all claims to social status dissolved and in which his father's fecklessness had nearly drowned him. But if Dickens was a writer with whom aesthetics can have nothing to do, since he deliberately had nothing to do with aesthetics, he is, all the same, a genius, and out of these limitations and from these fears he distilled more good fun and simple excitement than any other writer in English.

George Eliot

The publication of the first three of the six volumes of George Eliot's correspondence, which Professor Gordon S. Haight has been preparing for more than twenty years, is a strange and rather awful event. By the end of the third volume, or at mid-passage, the work has reached page 1366, and a number of doubts about the scale of the enterprise and the values involved are stirring in the detached reader's mind. As if aware of some of the questions that may be asked, the syndics of the Yale University Press have ornamented the dust jacket of Volume I with a justificatory quotation from Cardinal Newman, that "For arriving at the inside of things, the publication of letters is the true method." While this is no doubt true in saintly, innocent, and emotional circles, it fails to cover the three large groups of a more calculating nature—those who abide by the rule of never setting pen to paper if their emotions are involved, those who approach the writing table as the chess player approaches the chessboard, and those who use ink as the cuttlefish does, emitting large black clouds of it as a protective device. It is hard to say in which of these groups George Eliot belongs, but on the strength of the contents of these volumes the second, and most deliberately calculating, one seems the right choice.

The first letters date from her late teens and early twenties, and they are heavy with nonconformist cant and the earnest priggishness of youthful uncertainty. "I do not wonder you are pleased with Pascal; his thoughts may be returned to the palate again and again with increasing rather than diminished relish. I have highly enjoyed Hannah More's letters; the contemplation of so blessed a character as hers is very salutary." "I wonder if you have read Mr. Williams's account of his missionary enterprises in the South Seas. . . . I think I may venture to say that it could not fail to interest any person of taste to say nothing of religion." "I have just begun the Life of Wilberforce and I am expecting a rich treat from it. There is a similarity, if I may compare myself with such a man, between his temptations or rather besetments and my own that makes his experience very interesting to me." Block by block, the reputation for a wholly serious piety is built up, and though there are occasional revelations of the truth, they are almost entirely inadvertent disclosures of the toxic qualities of bigotry:

We have had an oratorio at Coventry lately, Braham, Phillips, Mrs. Knyvett and Mrs. Shaw, the last I think I shall attend. I am not fitted to decide on the question of the propriety or lawfulness of such exhibitions of talent and so forth because I have no soul for music. "Happy is he that condemneth not himself in that thing which he alloweth" but for my part I humbly conceive it to be little less than blasphemy for such words as "Now then we are ambassadors for Christ" to be taken on the lips of such a man as Braham (a Jew too!). I am a tasteless person but it would not cost me any regrets if the only music heard in our land were that of strict worship, nor can I think a pleasure that involves the devotion of all the time and powers of an immortal being to the acquirement of

an expertness in so useless an accomplishment can be quite pure
or elevating in its tendency.

This exhibition of provincialism leads up to a fine piece
of rationalization, dated February, 1839, which foreshad-
ows George Eliot's mature accomplishments. The problem
is that of the novel, which, according to her, is a worldly,
got-up thing, as unjustifiable as the oratorio:

As to the discipline our minds receive from the perusal of
fictions I can conceive none that is beneficial but may be attained by that of history. . . . Religious novels are more hate-
ful to me than merely worldly ones. They are a sort of Centaur
or Mermaid and like other monsters that we do not know how
to class should be destroyed for the public good as soon as
born. The weapons of the Christian warfare were never
sharpened at the forge of romance. Domestic fictions as they
come more within the range of imitation seem more dangerous.
For my part I am ready to sit down and weep at the impos-
sibility of my understanding or barely knowing even a fraction
of the sum of objects that present themselves for our contemplation in books and in life. Have I then any time to spend
on things that never existed?

The difficulty was that she enjoyed reading novels, Sir
Walter Scott's in particular. So the argument is unwound
that there is a special class of "persons of perceptions so
quick, memories so eclectic and retentive, and minds so
comprehensive" that nothing less than omnivorous reading
can satisfy them. It happens, too, that people frequently
make literary allusions in conversation, and it is one's social
duty to be able to pick these up. Further, sad and valuable
moral lessons are to be learned from the lives of authors,
notably Sir Walter Scott's ("the spiritual sleep of that man

was awful; he does not at least betray if he felt anything like a pang of conscience"). It is necessary to read their novels in order to appreciate the full weight of the moral lessons. When the subject is closed, it is satisfyingly clear that it is perfectly possible to be a novel reader without being an ordinary novel reader. It is an attractive dialectic method, with the great practical advantage of allowing one to do anything and everything ordinary people do without sacrificing the status of a superior moral being. As time went on, George Eliot was to make increasingly effective use of it.

Although the course of her development from this point is tortuous, it is fairly easy to follow through her letters. The religious doubt that succeeded her early piety opened the way to Unitarian rationalism, rationalism opened the way to bogus scientific interests such as phrenology, and phrenology opened the way to Comte's Religion of Humanity and to Feuerbach. What is almost completely invisible in the letters is the line of conduct the high-toned arguments screen.

From 1844 to 1846, George Eliot was solemnly wrapped up in the task of translating Strauss's *Life of Jesus* from the German, in apparent ignorance of the fact that it had already been translated in 1841 and widely distributed. Whether her accomplishment was necessary or not, it got her into some astonishing scrapes. The original sponsor of her translation was a Dr. Brabant, of Devizes, whose daughter had completed only two chapters before she got married. George Eliot was brought in to complete the task and to take the daughter's place in the Doctor's home. She arrived in Devizes at the beginning of November of 1843, and at first all went well; she wrote to a friend in delight:

I have been feasting my eyes on the Library this morning, and Dr. Brabant insists that I shall consider that my room. What name do you think I have been baptized withal? Rather a learned pun, Deutera, which *means* second and *sounds* a little like daughter. . . . I like Mrs. B. She talks so *neatly* and is so perfectly polite. A dose of precision, *not* preciseness, will be the best thing in the world for me. Dr. B's habits are of that regular and simple kind that always indicate a healthy mind. He does not even sit in an easy chair.

By the middle of the month a solid bliss had been achieved:

I am in little heaven here, Dr. Brabant being its archangel. . . . Mrs. Brabant is a most affectionate amiable being. . . . I have just written to Father to beg for a longer leave of absence than I had thought of when I came.

The first hint of trouble, though of its nature rather than of its coming, is in a letter dated November 24th:

Dr. Brabant spoils me for everyone else, and the Trennung from such a companion will be very painful. He really is a finer character than you think. Beautifully sincere, conscientious, and benevolent and every thing besides that one would have one's friends to be.

Six days later the *Trennung* was upon her, and, her boxes packed, she was writing to announce the sad fact that she was coming home:

We shall soon, I hope, be talking to each other "under your eyes" for I have just written to my good Mary telling her that I intend to be at the Coventry station by 9 o'clock on Monday evening. . . . I do not know whether to be glad or sorry, so I have come to a compromise with the contending feelings, and mean to indulge my grief at parting with my precious friends here till I reach home, and then let joy take complete possession.

There is no clue here at all to what had happened. What *had* happened was that Mrs. Brabant had neatly and precisely, if not perfectly amiably, delivered an ultimatum. George Eliot was to leave the house at once and not to return; if she did, Mrs. Brabant would go. Dr. Brabant, who had cheerfully made the most of George Eliot's inexperience in getting up the flirtation, passively allowed her to be put out. To quiet his conscience, he permitted her to go on with the translation of the *Life of Jesus* on her own.

When it was at last finished, it led her into the remarkable London establishment maintained at 142 Strand by John Chapman. He had not always been a publisher; he had, indeed, been apprenticed to a watchmaker, had been mysteriously occupied in the Colonies and "abroad," had practiced for a time, though unqualified, as a surgeon in Derby, and had at last come, by accident, to publishing. In Derby he had married money and written *Human Nature: A Philosophical Exposition of the Divine Institution of Reward and Punishment.* The activities were not wholly unrelated, since as soon as he had the money he took off for London to get the thesis published, if necessary at his own expense. In his search for a compliant publisher, he came across a sickly firm that had done itself no good by establishing a reputation as the leading Unitarian press in England, and, learning that it was going out of business, he bought it. He set himself up as a publisher at 142 Strand, a combined place of business and residence. It was too large for the Chapmans, and they converted it into a lodging house.

By the time George Eliot went there to live, some time

after her translation had been accepted, it had become a bizarre establishment. At the center of it was a *ménage à trois* composed of John Chapman, his wife, and a Miss Tilley, who was nominally helping with the children. These ladies were suspicious of George Eliot, since they had ground to fear that she was taking the place of a Miss Eliza Lynn, another of Mr. Chapman's authors, who had lately been a fourth party in the ménage, and when George Eliot sat down at the splendidly patriarchal dinner table over which Mr. Chapman presided (at which were seated his wife, his mistress, a number of lodgers, and some junior employees of the firm), Miss Tilley went into action. George Eliot retired to her room feeling "very poorly." Chapman made her his mistress shortly thereafter, and the household became a fine disorder of scenes, explanations, partings, and reconciliations. He had what was manifestly a delightful time playing each woman off against the two others and contriving devices to get all three to put up with the situation, while convincing himself that he was enduring a martyrdom. He complained to his diary that his concurrent attempt to adopt vegetarianism was being frustrated and that his moral nature was being overlaid. It was Miss Tilley's physical appeal for Chapman that finally led to George Eliot's departure from the household. After uselessly making scenes in a bottle factory and other unsuitable places, Miss Tilley at last adopted the practical measure of denying Chapman her person. "I would do anything in reason to restore her," he wrote in his diary. He thought it over for a moment or two, and then, with unusual honesty, crossed out "in reason." George Eliot was eased out by a course of readings in Thomas a Kempis, by profound discussions of sexual ethics, and at last by a "solemn and holy vow which will henceforth bind us to the right."

George Eliot came before long to realize just what "the right" amounted to, and consoled herself for having so very elaborately been made a fool of by attempting to annex Herbert Spencer, the author of *Social Statics*. He was, however, designed by nature to be a bachelor, and though she did all she could to compromise him he evaded entanglement. When this episode was over, she drifted out of the curious establishment in the Strand and into the orbit of an even odder one in Bayswater. It was inhabited by Mr. and Mrs. George Henry Lewes, Mr. and Mrs. Thornton Hunt, and Mrs. Hunt's two unmarried sisters. What gave it its unusual flavor was that four of Mrs. Lewes' six children were by her husband and two by Mr. Hunt. Lewes was a jolly, bouncy man who sported a raffish handle-bar mustache and affected a slightly idiosyncratic version of evening dress day and night. He was popular in some circles and notorious in others for his vulgar stories and for discussing in mixed company such things as free love and the anatomical charms of women who attracted him, but his improper novels were universally deplored. He fell in love with George Eliot and she with him, and presently they ran away to Germany. They lived together outside the bond of marriage until he died, over twenty years later.

The translation of this action, which would in the case of an ordinary person be a mere matter of deciding that adultery was worth the social consequences, into an altruistic act of moral courage was a feat of intellectual legerdemain for which George Eliot was well equipped. From the time she entered the Lewes circle until she ran off with him, her letters are full of references to Feuerbach's *Essence of Christianity*, a work she was translating into English and pressing John Chapman to publish with ferocious determination. He was in financial difficulties, and he knew the book would lose money, but she was adamant. And she thrust the book and its ideas upon her friends. Among the truths Feuerbach was forwarding was that "Love is God Himself . . . not a visionary, imaginary love—no! a real love, a love which has flesh and blood." According to him, marriage expressed the divine by means of the sexual relationship, provided that it was a truly moral marriage in which the only bond was love within perfect freedom. Ordinary marriages—in which the bond was "merely an external restriction, not the voluntary, contented self-restriction of love," marriages that were not "spontaneously concluded, spontaneously willed, and self-sufficing"—were not truly moral ones. It was thus perfectly clear that Mr. and Mrs. Lewes were not married and that he was free to take off with George Eliot. He had, in fact, an obligation, since it was the social duty of enlightened persons to set examples of moral conduct. It was the old story of the problem of novel reading, and the dialectic conjuring trick produced the required result in the same way; it was possible to be an adulterer without being an ordinary adulterer, to be George Eliot without in the least resembling Miss Tilley. The letters she wrote immediately after she had bolted with Lewes are pathetic in their belief that the conjuring trick can persuade the external world:

It is possible that you have already heard a report prevalent in London that Mr. Lewes has "run away" from his wife and family. I wish you to be in possession of the facts which will enable you to contradict this report whenever it reaches you. Since we left England he has been in constant correspondence with his wife. . . . I have seen all the correspondence between them, and it has assured me that his conduct as a husband has been not only irreproachable, but generous and self-sacrificing to a degree far beyond any standard fixed by the world. This is the simple truth, and no flattering picture drawn by my partiality.

After six months, it was clear to her that only a superior being could understand the motives and acts of another superior being:

I can dilate on nothing now. I will only say that if you knew everything, we should probably be much nearer agreement even as to the details of conduct than you suppose. In the mean time, believe no one's representations about me, for there is not a *single person* who is in a position to make a true representation.

It was this lack of understanding that finally made George Eliot a novelist. The first impetus came from Lewes and was conceived in kindness; he realized that they would face ostracism, and that a woman of her active mind would find loneliness boring. He proposed a novel to her to fill in the time until the scandal blew over. She did not respond to the suggestion until she had had an ugly shock. John Chapman made an effort to persuade a young friend of hers to live with him, and in the course of his argument he had put forth the example of Lewes and George Eliot as a couple whose happiness was unclouded by their lack of marriage lines. Eliot was shaken to find that a truly moral marriage could be presented in this light, and felt the urgent need for a fuller explanation of her principles

than the bare action was able to supply. Besides, she and
Lewes were desperately poor; one day when they were
walking in the park, Lewes had burst out with the cry "We
should live much better than we do, we should have beer
at lunch," and there was not enough money even for that,
with beer at a penny a pint. The novel is, of course, the
only profitable instrument available to the moralist, so it
was clearly fiction that was called for. And so George Eliot
began to write novels.

It is hard from this distance to decide why the novels
were instantly best-sellers, or why George Eliot so rapidly
became one of Queen Victoria's favorite writers, since they
are so earnestly and gracelessly written. But this was precisely their strength when they were fresh and new; they
were manifestly entirely serious, and they could be read
on a Sunday without raising any suspicion of Sabbath-
breaking. Their basis is always what modern critics have
called "the moral imagination," and the reader is never allowed to forget it. This absence of frivolity is, however,
not in itself enough to account for George Eliot's past and
revived reputation, and for such devotional acts as the publication of this edition of her letters. There is something
more. In exchange for submitting to the remorseless process of improvement, the reader receives a certain compensation; the George Eliot dialectic of self-justification transferred to the field of fiction proves to be one of the most
effective devices for flattering mediocrity that have yet
been invented.

George Eliot's most successful and still most popular
novel, *Middlemarch*, begins with an odd little preface that
most people skip, since it is concerned with Saint Theresa
of Avila, who seems to have very little to do with the mat-

ters in hand, the rather muddled feelings of a lady called
Dorothea for certain gentlemen. The point of introducing
the subject of Saint Theresa is revealed in the closing para-
graphs of the book:

Certainly those determining acts of her life were not ideally
beautiful. They were the mixed result of young and noble impulse struggling amidst the conditions of an imperfect social
state, in which great feeling will often take the aspect of error,
and great faith the aspect of illusion. For there is no creature
whose inward being is so strong that it is not greatly determined by what lies outside it. A new [Saint] Theresa will
hardly have the opportunity of reforming a conventual life,
any more than a new Antigone will spend her heroic piety by
daring all for the sake of a brother's burial: the medium in
which their ardent deeds took shape is forever gone. But we
insignificant people with our daily words and acts are preparing the lives of many Dorotheas, some of which may present
a far sadder sacrifice than that of the Dorothea whose story
we know.

Her finely touched spirit had still its fine issues, though they
were not widely visible. Her full nature, like that river of
which Cyrus broke the strength, spent itself in channels which
had no great name on earth. But the effect of her being on
those around her was incalculably diffusive: for the growing
good of the world is partly dependent on unhistoric acts; and
that things are not so ill with you and me as they might have
been, is half owing to the number who lived faithfully a hidden
life, and rest in unvisited tombs.

There is no need to point out the coziness of this kind of
thing. It not only puts the business of running away with
Mr. Lewes in the name of the truly moral marriage on a
footing with the acts of such splendid creatures as Antigone, but it also allows everyone who has followed his in-

clinations at any time to do the same, even if his inclinations have led him to do nothing out of the way. What one sees in—or, rather, through—these letters is the slow perfection of a technique of self-deception that in the end equipped its possessor to become a perfect supplier of soft solder to *l'homme moyen sensuel*, the swamped and ignoble Tartufe of industrial society. But fascinating as the documents are from a sociological and psychological point of view, it is baffling to see them offered as exhibits of the working of the mind of a creative artist. In their involved lack of candor (not one is an uncalculated declaration from the heart) one recognizes what the true artist instinctively discards even in his weakest moments—the desire to force the truth to conform to a preconceived ideal by an effort of will.

Note: Professor Haight took strong exception to this essay, and was particularly incensed by my statement that George Eliot had been John Chapman's mistress: it was his view that there was no evidence to support it. We had a brief discussion on the point in the columns of the *New Yorker* in which he evidently felt himself constrained by the house rules of the magazine, and the matter came to no more than a preliminary exchange. I myself also felt constrained on this occasion though for another reason; the evidence, which Professor Haight himself had supplied me with, was of a kind that is hard to deal with explicitly in the pages of a "family magazine." In 1940 the Yale University Press published Professor Haight's *George Eliot and John Chapman*, the latter half of which consists of John Chapman's diaries for 1851 and 1860. Over the entry of Sunday 12

January 1851 there is a plus sign followed by the notation
10 A.M.; a footnote explains this:

"An initial (E) before the cross has been erased. These
crosses, appearing at regular intervals in the Diary, refer to
Elisabeth's physical condition."

The reference is discreet, but the recurrence of these signs
at twenty-eight-day intervals makes it quite clear what
John Chapman was recording. On Saturday 18 January
1851 the entry M.PM appears in the same position, at the
head of the space allotted to that day, as the clinical note
about E. The note M.AM appears in a similar position on
Sunday 19 January. In both cases a later attempt has been
made to erase the entry. George Eliot was still Marian
Evans at that stage of her career and in the body of the
diary Chapman refers to her as "M" more often than not.
The presence of these two entries in the place in the diary
where Chapman kept the records of his sexual life seems
to me conclusive.

The attentive reader will notice that in this essay I first
mention Feuerbach in connection with Comte and his Religion of Humanity, and later say something of Feuerbach's
ideas as they relate to George Eliot's behavior without mentioning Comte. Exigencies of space accounted for the dis-
appearance of a brief account of the Religion of Humanity
with its central conception of a self-elected elite, privileged
by their nobility of spirit to do what they fancied. As this
collection is of the *New Yorker* essays as they appeared,
for better or worse, I don't feel justified in resurrecting the
passage now. The flaw is there to record a technical failure
on my part in not writing within the confines of the medium, and I have let it stand and have drawn attention to

it for the light it may throw on the technical problems that come up in writing this kind of criticism. There is a most brilliant account of Comte's ideas in Noel Annan's life of Leslie Stephen. This is not only the best biography known to me written in English by anyone of my generation, but it is also one of the best studies of the influence of ideas on a man's life that exists. It gives an unequaled picture of English intellectual life in the last century, it is beautifully and wittily written, and it is illustrated with some extremely pleasant photographs of Virginia Woolf's parents and of Henry James. Stephen was Virginia Woolf's father, and figures in *To the Lighthouse*. It is a matter of surprise and distress to me that this example of English academic criticism at its very best should not, so far, have found an American publisher. It is the sort of permanently valuable and dubiously commercial thing, one would think, which university presses exist to print.

Emile Zola

The Kill is an opulent translation, dating from 1895, of *La Curée*, Emile Zola's second novel in the series devoted to the Rougon-Macquart clan. It exhibits him at his censorious worst, pitching into the sins of Paris in the style in which the old-time preachers of the Bible belt fulminated against the wickedness of a New York they had never seen. The target of Zola's moralizing was the society of the Second Empire, and the section of it to which he turned his attention in this particular novel was the one that had been enriched by the Haussmannization of Paris. Zola, as Mr. Angus Wilson declares in a preface to the present edition, was entirely unacquainted with this carefully selected subject matter. He based his story on "the blue books of the State Auditor's office, the fashion columns of the newspapers, the sales inventories of rich houses, and the catalogue of contents of the hothouses of the Jardin des Plantes." Mr. Wilson adds that courage was required to write the novel with this slender equipment, but Zola supplied another explanation for his ability to produce it. It was a matter not of having courage but of surrendering to a compulsion, the nature of which was thoroughly understood by Zola himself. In advocating continence for the literary man, Zola once said:

134

The chaste writer can be immediately recognized by the fierce virility of his touch. He is filled with desires as he writes, and these desires prompt the outbursts in his great masterpieces.

The Kill, apparently the fruit of prolonged abstinence, describes the love affair of handsome, effeminate Maxime and his pretty young stepmother, Renée, a woman who, it appears as early as page 9, is unusually responsive to landscape:

Renée, satiated as she was, experienced a singular sensation of illicit desire at the sight of this landscape that had become unrecognizable, of this bit of nature, so worldly and artificial, which the great vibrating darkness transformed into a sacred grove, one of the ideal glades in whose recesses the gods of old concealed their Titanic loves, their adulteries, and their divine incests.

This is not a mere passing fancy inspired by a particular grove; another part of the Bois de Boulogne, on page 11, sends her again:

And an immense temptation rose from the empty space, from the copses asleep in the shadow on either side of the avenue, from the noise of wheels and from the gentle oscillation that filled her with a delicious torpor. A thousand tremulous emotions passed over her flesh; dreams unrealized, nameless delights, confused longings, all the monstrous voluptuousness that a drive home from the Bois under a paling sky can infuse into a woman's worn heart.

Poor Renée is not destined, one can see, to be happy or to know tranquillity. Even the architecture of her husband's house is against her; its first appearance, on page 14, can only be called inflammatory:

Around the windows and along the cornices ran swags of flowers and branches; there were balconies shaped like baskets full of blossoms, and supported by great naked women with straining hips, with breasts jutting out before them; then, here and there, were planted fanciful escutcheons, clusters of fruit, roses, every flower that it is possible for stone or marble to represent. The higher the eye ascended, the more the building burst into blossom. Around the roof ran a balustrade on which stood, at equal intervals, urns blazing with flames of stone. And there, between the bull's-eye windows of the attics, which opened on to an incredible confusion of fruit and foliage, mantled the crowning portions of this stupendous scheme of decoration, the pediments of the turrets, amid which reappeared the great naked women, playing with apples, attitudinizing amidst sheaves of rushes.

This bizarre construction, as might be feared, has a conservatory attached to it. In the warmth of its artificial landscape, Maxime and Renée are presently snuggling on a large black bearskin and watching botanical manifestations that few other observers anywhere have ever been lucky enough to see:

Around them the palm-trees and the tall Indian bamboos rose up towards the arched roof, where they bent over and mingled their leaves with the staggering attitudes of exhausted lovers. Lower down the ferns, the pterides, the alsophilas, were like green ladies, with ample skirts trimmed with symmetrical flounces, who stood mute and motionless at the edge of the pathway awaiting love. By their side the twisted red-streaked leaves of the begonias and the white spear-headed leaves of the caladiums furnished a vague series of bruises and pallors, which the lovers could not explain to themselves, though at times they discerned curves as of hips and knees, prone on the ground be-

neath the brutality of ensanguined kisses. And the plantain-
trees, bending under the weight of their fruit, spoke to them
of the rich fecundity of the soil, while the Abyssinian euphor-
bias, of whose prickly, deformed, tapering stems, covered with
loathly excrescences, they could catch glimpses in the shadow,
seemed to sweat out sap, the over-flowing flux of this fiery
gestation. But, by degrees, as their glances penetrated into the
corners of the conservatory, the darkness became filled with
a more furious debauch of leaves and stalks; they were not able
to distinguish on the stages between the marantas, soft as velvet,
the gloxinias, purple-belled, the dracoenas, resembling blades
of old lacquer; it was one round dance of living plants pursu-
ing one another with unsatiated fervor.

  This would be good fooling if Zola had any sense of fun,
but he is a stern moralist with a hatred of all pleasures, and
of sexuality above everything, and he is writing in complete
seriousness. This is supposed to be a straightforward picture
of corruption, the corruption typical of the *nouveau riche*,
or, more simply, of successful businessmen and their wives.
The financial operations that supply the funds for these
shenanigans are described with loving care, as if they, too,
were diabolically sinful, but they appear to be real-estate
speculations of a fairly common kind. The implication that
this inevitably leads to sin on bearskins seems absurd. When
Renée rounds out the book by dying of meningitis, one
suspects that it is not she who is corrupt but her creator,
and that she is given the beating she gets for being attractive, or for being the embodiment of what is attractive, and
for arousing something in him that he dislikes and fears.
It was not, after all, Renée but Zola who saw such a remarkable vision of the harvest fields in *La Faute de l'Abbé
Mouret*:

By night, this burning countryside took on strange, passionate postures. It slept, its dress in indecent disorder, twisted, its limbs flung apart, while heavy, warm sighs were wafted upwards, the powerful scent of a woman asleep and in sweat.

In the same book, one discovers a parallel vision, not of an artificial paradise in a hothouse but of the natural order:

From the most secret recesses, from the pools of sunlight, from the patches of shadow, an animal odor mounted, of all the universe on heat. The whole of this swarming life shuddered in travail. Beneath each leaf, an insect was conceiving; in every tuft of grass, a family was growing; flies in the air, clinging together, could not wait to settle. The specks of invisible life that infest matter, the atoms of matter themselves, loved, mated, made the soil heave with sensuality, turned the park into one great orgy.

The phrase "that infest matter" is a giveaway that leads one to recognize both in the passage and in the body of Zola's work a private neurosis and a source of inspiration shared with the hell-fire preachers—a terror of life, and a sour envy of those with the courage to live it.

There is more light on this point in the revealing essay by Mr. Angus Wilson that serves as an introduction to the new edition of Zola's *Restless House* (*Pot-Bouille*), an essay which does a good deal to account for the particular emptiness and aridity of the new school of English novel-writing of the Kingsley Amis and John Wayne persuasion. Mr. Wilson, whose method and line of approach owe more to Zola than to anyone else, explains that a bitter discontent was hag-riding Zola when he wrote *Pot-Bouille*. "The novelist felt increasing need to project this personal misery

into literary form—the writer's instinctive means of self-
healing," he declares. Mr. Wilson goes on to accept Zola's
picture of bourgeois Paris, seen through eyes glazed with
pain and distress, as a valid one. It is a city in which all
kitchens smell of rancid butter, in which everybody wears
soiled underclothes, and in which nobody finds sex a source
of pleasure.

Gradually the truth about these homes is revealed—women
nourishing themselves upon the romance of fifth-rate novels,
women hysteric with sexual dissatisfaction, women who have
come to regard their husbands as automata to be pushed up the
social ladder, daughters who hate the mothers who are schem-
ing to find them profitable marriages as sterile as their own.
. . . Whatever the slight material and social differences that
separate them, differences over which they sweat so much
blood of envy and pride, all are living the same lie—a lie of
polite social talk, little card parties, small family dances, pre-
tentious musical evenings.

This murky hell is, of course, exactly the same one we
see in the conversation pictures of Renoir and in the early
work, luminous with petty pleasures, of Vuillard and Bon-
nard. There is a possibility, which some writer should someday entertain, that people enjoy small talk, cards, dancing,
and musical evenings, and enjoy them in the family circle—
even when they have occasional sexual adventures outside
it—because they love each other, on the whole, more than
they irritate or depress each other. Zola's picture of life in
a Parisian apartment house has an electric vitality, but it is
grotesque in its solid concentration on its physical and
moral squalor. The service staircase is always referred to as
a sewer, and the courtyard onto which the kitchens and
maids' rooms open is pictured as a cesspool of vile talk. The

front part of the house is worse. Zola makes no exceptions in describing life in his apartment house: "If you've been in one of them you've been in all. They're all pig sties." Common experience, though, no matter how finical the observer, or how cynical, suggests that this assessment of middle-class behavior is too sweeping. One is always running into men of that class who seem to like their wives and are honest in their relations with them. They do not appear to differ radically from their grandparents, many of whom have left behind memories of more than brief flashes of happiness and lives not altogether corrupt. The contemporary critics who derided Zola's realism as a love of the nasty may not have been merely mouthpieces of bourgeois hypocrisy; it may be that their reaction was a healthy one and that what they disliked so much was not his honesty but a fundamental flaw in his writing. One suspects that the new English neo-realists have accepted the flaw as a virtue. It is the same flaw Sherwood Anderson thought he detected in Henry James:

You may be interested to know my reactions to some solid weeks of James reading—the feeling of him as a man who never found anyone to love, who did not dare love. I really can't care much for any character after he gets through with it; he, in short, takes my love from me too. I've a fancy—can it be true that he is the novelist of the haters? Oh, the thing infinitely refined and carried far into the field of intellectuality, as skillful haters find out how to do.

Machado de Assis

Machado de Assis, the Brazilian author of *Epitaph of a Small Winner*, is a pleasant, if belated, discovery for English-speaking readers. His excellent translator, Dr. William L. Grossman of New York University, who is an expert on transportation law and economics, came on his work by chance a few years ago, in the course of learning Portuguese while he was serving as head of the economics department of a Brazilian college. His translation is a labor of love in which he communicates the pleasure of his lucky find. In an admirable preface, Dr. Grossman tells us about Machado, who seems to have been a remarkable figure. He was born in Rio de Janeiro in 1839, the son of a mulatto house painter and a Portuguese immigrant. His mother died soon after he was born, and his father not long after a second marriage. He was brought up in poverty by his stepmother. He received a sketchy education, picking up a smattering in five years at the indifferent public schools, getting something a little better during the brief period his stepmother was a cook at a girls' school, and teaching himself, in his adolescence, while he worked in a printshop as a typesetter and proofreader. In his early years, he learned French from a French baker, and in later life he taught himself English. Weakened by rickets in childhood, myopic, and cursed with epilepsy, Machado had a solid foundation for hypochondria, and from his thirties onward invalidism touched the pattern of his existence. It was not possible in his day in Brazil to make a living as a professional writer, and for most of his life he worked in government offices (proving again, as do the lives of so many eighteenth- and nineteenth-century writers, the cultural benefits afforded by an unreformed and technically inefficient civil service). In spite of these handicaps, Machado's collected works run to thirty-one volumes of epic poetry, lyric poetry, plays, short stories, novels, criticism, and journalism.

Dr. Grossman is guarded about the quality of the bulk of this material, and it is perhaps ominous that it earned Machado, and by a unanimous vote, the presidency of the Brazilian Academy of Letters in 1897. It was a period of unparalleled literary chauvinism, and it was marked by efforts of the stuffier literary personalities in every country to establish imitations of the Académie Française in which carefully chosen and reliably uncreative writers could meet in the warmth of mutual admiration in order to critically inflate one of their older and more exhausted colleagues to the point at which he could be hailed as the national Goethe. If, however, Machado was late in life the Manzoni or the Walter Scott of Brazil, and an ornament of its official culture, he enjoyed in his fortieth year a moment of creative clarity in which he was much better than that. On recovering from a long bout of illness, he cleansed his work of its conventionally romantic elements and wrote—or, rather, dictated to his wife—a novel that embodies all that he had learned from his sensitive and intelligent studies of French and English literary models. This was his *Epitaph of a Small Winner*. Superficially it is a formal exercise in imitating the technique Sterne perfected in *Tristram Shandy*, but it is Sterne's technique strengthened with the psychological realism of the French novel. This combination of alien influences in a necessarily provincial milieu could easily have produced something pedantic and dead, but Machado had a psychological insight of his own, an incisive wit, and, surprisingly, an aristocratic toughness of mind that saved him from any imitative woodenness. *Epitaph of a Small Winner* has the experimental and inventive vitality that one associates with the writing of the 'twenties, and it seems to belong much more in spirit to that lively period than to the 'eighties, in which it was first published. If it has to be given a category, it should be placed alongside such successful modern *jeux d'esprit* as Hemingway's *The Torrents of Spring* and Montherlant's *Pity for Women* —jokes that are all the better for being savage and, like all good jokes, wholly serious.

Hemingway, in *The Torrents of Spring*, romped in high spirits with an idea that comes up again and again in the work of Sherwood Anderson and D. H. Lawrence—that the life of the instincts is superior to the life of the intellect, that the primitive tribal life is nearer the uncorrupted source than civilized life, and that tribal values are therefore superior to civilized values. He took this idea, which inverts the white-supremacy idea, and ran it to earth in its nest of fallacies simply by applying broad comedy effects to it—notably in a scene in an Indian club in which a white man "passing" is unmasked and thrown out into the street. The book demolishes attitudes such as those in Lawrence's *The Plumed Serpent*, and it is not only one of the best and most effective pieces of literary criticism produced in the 'twenties but one of the better, and enduring, literary jokes of a lighthearted time. It may be added that it was a dangerous joke for Hemingway to make, since if it blows Lawrence's noble Mexicans sky-high, it also ruffles the furry chests of a great many of his own more dumbly virile heroes.

Machado's joke has the same slightly suicidal edge, since its attack on romantic idealism is so absolute that it can be taken for a nihilistic attack on all forms of belief, including the values that produced it. Dr. Grossman does so take it, and refers to Machado as "perhaps the most completely disenchanted writer in Occidental literature," but this seems to disregard the very deliberate, classical use of irony that is part of Machado's technique. Montherlant can be dismissed as an ugly-minded writer who despises women, if *Pity for Women* is read with the assumption that its central character speaks for its author and that the book's core is satisfaction with a dreary kind of male egotism but it is fairly clear that an ironist is at work and that Montherlant is being as savage about his hero's attitude to women as he is about women. Behind the hero's pity for women for being such a low grade of animal that their instincts can always take over their lives, and always to their disadvantage, there is the author's pity for the hero's intellectual deformity. He is a rake in the grip of one set of compulsions, and the author's irony is focussed on his unawareness of the fact and his disgust with women for being trapped in another set of compulsions. The ironist constantly uses a double-edged weapon, and he generally cannot resist giving an edge to the hilt as well, so that anyone who grasps the thing in the wrong way will get a third cut from it; the attack on the naïve reader is just as strong as it is on the targets inside the book. Machado seems to be playing this rather elaborate teasing game. The final words of *Epitaph of a Small Winner* sum up the extent to which its hero, Braz

Cubas, is ahead of the game at the end of his life: "I found that I had a small surplus. . . . I had no progeny, I transmitted to no one the legacy of our misery." To Dr. Grossman, this is a definite statement of the author's absolute pessimism, but it can be read as a diagnosis of what is, or was, incurably wrong with Braz Cubas.

Braz Cubas is, *mutatis mutandis*, a Brazilian George Apley, an average member of a fortunate class of people. He has enough money to free him from all pressures and an almost unlimited opportunity to make his life what he chooses. He lives timidly and uncertainly on the fringes of literature, always intending to write something really good someday, and on the fringes of politics, always intending to make a splash someday. His complete lack of will or tenacity, and of intellectual discipline, insures that his life boils down to a series of dim affairs with women in which he flirts in a scared way but with a certain intensity of feeling. Machado follows him through his ineffectual romances, ruthlessly describing their empty reality, and allows him to make these shallow, negative experiences the basis of his nihilist philosophy of despair. The contrasts between his intellectual self-importance and his incapacity for living produce some extraordinary effects, of both comedy and pathos. In his first affair, he is taken for what the traffic will bear by a hardheaded little gold-digger called Marcella. It is the only episode in his life that he really understands, because it all turns on the girl's simple appetite for hard cash. Love comes his way as a genuine emotion when he meets Eugenia, who loves him, but before it is too late he notices that she has a slight limp—she has limped from birth —she is a cripple—marry a cripple—impossible—he bolts in

a fright from the situation that has so nearly betrayed him
into a world of valid experience.

The remainder of his life is taken up with a long-drawn-
out adultery with the wife of a friend. This is described in
a series of tours de force of realistic writing, episodic and
exact. Everything superfluous is pared away, and only the
vital episodes are presented. Machado had a remarkably
sure sense of what was important—at least when he was
writing this novel—and the whole of the relationship is
there, from its origin to its last ramifications. In a sequence
of the briefest scenes, he shows the affair at the stage of
private rapture, shows it branching out and becoming the
subject of gossip, shows its effect on Braz Cubas' family and
on the local society. He shows, too, its diminution of intensity, its deterioration into habit, and its final extinction
under the weight of social expediency. It is an absorbing
story about that most deadly of diseases, the incapacity to
love, and about the intellectual dishonesty of the shallow-
hearted. When the affair has collapsed, and become so
meaningless that Braz Cubas can boast of its secret delights
in casual conversation (the death of the spirit is complete),
he settles into a cozy round of puttering and waiting to die
in the shade of his gray pessimism. To liven things up for
him, an old school friend, the most promising and brilliant
of his classmates, turns up, flat broke and a total failure,
but ready, all the same, to state a richly optimistic philosophy of existence—rather akin to Blake's and Whitman's—
called Humanitism, which has as its center an unlimited belief in the human power to create happiness and to enrich
life. Machado's ironic last chapters describe the way in
which the pallidly defeated Braz Cubas shelters and cher-
ishes his friend, whom he considers to be a lunatic. So does

Dr. Grossman, who takes it that Machado is laughing at the idea of the Nietzschean superman in the person of Braz Cubas' friend. It may be that he is right, but it does not seem likely that the wholly negativist outlook he attributes to Machado could have produced such a sparkling and enjoyable comedy. It is easier to believe that if Machado is in the book at all, he appears as the suspected friend; it takes a robust mind to write real tragedy in the form of comedy. Yet even if one has to disagree with Dr. Grossman about the content of the book, one can only be grateful to him for introducing a classic comedy of ideas, as fascinating as it is delightful, to the English language.

A Postscript—Oscar Wilde

Son of Oscar Wilde, Vyvyan Holland's account of his childhood and youth, is a story of intense unhappiness wantonly inflicted and of great courage and steadfastness. No matter how one feels about Oscar Wilde's homosexuality, it is surely beyond argument that neither his wife nor his two sons, Cyril and Vyvyan, aged ten and nine at the time of the scandal, should have been punished on that account. How any healthy-minded person could have felt anything but sympathy for these wholly innocent members of the family when the facts of the situation came out is difficult to imagine. It must have been hard enough for Mrs. Wilde to bear the money worries, the prolonged absences, and the inexplicable tensions generated in her home by her husband's relationship with Lord Alfred Douglas; it can only have been appalling to discover, when the matter came to court, that behind that relationship, which was comprehensible in terms of an overwhelming infatuation, was the moral ugliness of Mr. Taylor's squalid call house and its blackmailing habitués. Anyone close to her or in a position to help her should have wanted to do whatever was possible to shield her from further pain and distress. The incredible truth is, however, that everything was done to punish her for having loved Wilde and to implant a sense of guilt in the children.

In one of the more ironical passages in *De Profundis*,

Wilde turns from a discussion of the errors Douglas's mother made in bringing him up to express the hope that his own wife will not make the same mistakes in preparing her sons for life:

I told her that if she was frightened of facing the responsibilities of the life of another, though her own child, she should get a guardian to help her. That she has, I am glad to say, done. She has chosen Adrian Hope, a man of high birth and culture and fine character, her own cousin, whom you met once at Tite Street, and with him Cyril and Vyvyan have a good chance of a beautiful future.

It was not a good chance. The two small boys were packed off abroad while the scandal was at its height. They could see their father's name on the newsstand placards and in the headlines of the papers they occasionally glimpsed, but they were forbidden to mention his name. He had vanished into a blaze of notoriety, but no plausible explanation of why was ever given them. Cyril finally got hold of a newspaper and found out, but he could not bring himself to tell his younger brother, and the secret festered between them until it destroyed their friendship. They were thrown out of a Swiss hotel, with their mother, for bearing the name of Wilde, and presently their name was taken from them in a curiously primitive ceremony:

One day, shortly after our arrival at Bevaix, my brother and I were called into the dining room, which also served my uncle as a study. We were told to sit down and were then informed that in future our names would no longer be Wilde, but would be changed to Holland. And we were told to practice writing our new names, and were given some sort of document to sign. . . . At the same time we were told to forget that we had ever borne the name of Wilde and never to mention it to anyone. All our possessions were gone through to make certain that the name Wilde did not appear on any of them, and all our clothes were remarked. . . . It is significant that I do not remember my brother ever mentioning our father's name to me from that day onward.

After a few terms together at a school in Germany, the boys were separated lest anyone recognize them because of their Christian names. After their mother died and their guardian, backed by a council of relatives, had taken charge of them, they were not even allowed to spend their holidays with each other, and in a further exercise of primitive ritual they were made to think that their father was dead:

We were not told this in so many words, as that would have been a lie and I do not suppose that anyone in the family ever told a deliberate lie. But the impression was conveyed and we accepted it as a fact.

It was then thought safe to bring the two children home and put them in English schools. Vyvyan, by now twelve, returned in time for the autumn term, with the happy prospect of the Christmas holidays ahead of him. But none of his relatives would have him, so he spent the fortnight's vacation at a wind-swept summer resort near his school, in the care of one of its masters. The following Christmas would have been just as bleak had not a friend of his mother's taken him in. She was very old and could see him for only a few minutes each day, but she managed to give him more warmth and kindness than he had had from anyone else. A year later, he learned of his father's death, and when he went off to spend Christmas with a great-aunt he was wearing a black armband.

I had not been at my aunt's house for more than four minutes when my black armband was ripped away, and it was once
more impressed upon me that my life was not like that of other
boys and I could not go into mourning for my father. I was
given to understand that I could never make any sort of life
for myself in England, but must seek my fortune elsewhere.

The season of jollification and good will began happily
enough, but his innocent repetition of a rhyme with a double meaning had such dreadful consequences that it led him
to attempt suicide. This was deemed an indication that he
needed special attention, and this his family took care to
provide:

I spent most of the year 1901 in a salubrious town in the
Midlands, boarded out with a well-meaning gentleman who
had been the High Church Anglican incumbent of a very good
living in the West Country, but who had become a Roman
Catholic in middle age. With the loss of his living, my host also
lost his only source of income. Being married, with a wife living, he could not become a Catholic priest. So he compromised
by leading an ascetic life and spending a great part of the day
in reading the Catholic breviary. I imagine that the first part
of this program was not particularly difficult to adhere to. His
wife, poor woman, worn out by child-bearing and parochial
duties, was well past her prime; she had refused to adopt her
husband's new religion and became a dipsomaniac instead; with
whiskey at three shillings a bottle it was very difficult to prevent a determined woman from indulging her hobby.

The following year, Vyvyan went back to school, and
he finished up in excellent fashion, with an armful of prizes
and all ready to go on to Cambridge. His family sent him
to Switzerland for the summer to brush up his foreign lan-
guages at Dr. Kümmer's crammer, in Ouchy. At the end

of his term there, he experienced whiskey for the first time, at a farewell party. It went to his legs, and he had to be helped back to his aunt's house in the town, where he was boarding. She, being a good woman, spread the news to the rest of the family at once, and in a few days those who were truly fond of him were letting him know it:

My dear Vyvyan, I wonder if you realise how shocked and how distressed I am at the report of you that I have had from your Aunt Nellie: that you were brought home dead drunk on Saturday night by some men who picked you up in the street.

To think that I have to hear such a thing of you, Vyvyan, you who have had everything done for you to teach and help you to do right, you who know you have loving relations and friends who care immensely what you do, you to whom we have tried in every way to make up . . .

The tirade runs on at length in this vein. Vyvyan returned to England and to more homilies on sin and the need for repentance. He had to sit and watch the liquor in the house being ostentatiously locked up after every meal. It was a relief to escape to Cambridge (he wanted to go to Oxford, because his father had been there, and that was the reason for sending him to Cambridge) and to a siege of cramming for the Preliminary Examination. He sublimated his unhappiness in hard work under the watchful eye of his tutor, a kindly man who was so impressed by his seriousness that after a fortnight he abruptly spoke up: "Look here, there must be some mistake somewhere. When I first saw your guardian, he told me that you were a most difficult case, that you were idle, drank to excess, and frequented bad company." It was a turning point; the long-drawn-out attempt to cripple and warp the youth had failed. He had at last reached a domain of frankness and decency, in which there were many people who were proud to have known his father and who were glad to know him. His brother was not so fortunate, as the tormented letters Vyvyan quotes unhappily make clear:

All these years my great incentive has been to wipe that stain away; to retrieve, if may be, by some action of mine, a name no longer honoured in the land. The more I thought of this, the more convinced I became that, first and foremost, I must be a *man*. There was to be no cry of decadent artist, of effeminate aesthete, of weak-kneed degenerate. That is the first step. For that I have laboured; for that I have toiled.

This strange chronicle of sustained, cold cruelty to children is not a particularly elegant piece of writing, but it is nonetheless of considerable literary value. The fantastic behavior it describes is that of very ordinary people leading what is known as normal lives. As one reads it one is made to realize how timid the novelists of the time were in their description of the life around them, and how shallow the penetration of the novel still is. When one is confronted with the facts of such a situation as the one Vyvyan Holland so candidly presents, it is tempting to suspect that many of the recent efforts to steer the novel away from realism, on the pretext that the technique has been exhausted, are evasions rather than aesthetic developments. What was done to Vyvyan and Cyril Holland was the kind of thing that went on in the society from which Henry James gathered the material for his fragile webs of hint and suggestion; the contrast between the thin gruel of mystifications in *The Turn of the Screw* and the evil of the deliberate grinding away by this large group of hearty middle-class people at the happiness and the natural, instinctive appetite for life of Wilde's children is an enlightening one. And it is worth comparing what these real children learned with *What Maisie Knew*, for this confrontation shows that Jamesian psychology bears on something other than human behavior and that the questions it so delicately explores—and at such length—are prudently selected substitutes for brutal actualities. The horrid core of the Wilde story is that Oscar Wilde never did anything in his life as wicked as the things that were done ostensibly to shield his children from the consequences of the exposure of his private affairs. The evil people in his story were the nominal defenders of the decencies—the lunatic Marquess of Queensberry, who hated his former wife and their son, Lord Alfred Douglas; the lawyers and policemen who allowed themselves to become the agents of his hatred; the newspapermen who battened on the story—all those people to whom the scandal brought the opportunity of giving pain, and who inflicted it without stopping to think what the results might be. The fascination of the Wilde case—to the literature of which Vyvyan Holland's book is a most important addition—is that it demonstrates the absurdity of the literary convention which identifies evil with sexual irregularity, and illuminates that more deadly brand of wickedness which wears a shining morning face and always claims the very best intentions.

Hugh Walpole

Mr. Rupert Hart-Davis's *Hugh Walpole* is an example of the official biography, sanctioned and approved by the executors and near relatives of the departed, that has come to be part of the obsequies of a successful literary man. The form, it must be confessed, is not especially rewarding, and such biographies too often remind one of the funerary rituals of certain primitive nomadic tribes, which, when they have buried one of their members, pile stones upon the grave in order to weigh down the ghost and to make sure that it stays put until it has lost its power to harm the living. The official biographer is, as a rule, required to clamp his subject's public reputation into place, like a white marble monument, over the untidiness of his private personality, to hold that personality down until time has softened and dissolved both its pettier and its grosser aspects. Mr. Hart-Davis's biography is, however, something of an exception, partly because he is a great deal more sensible than most of the writers entrusted with constructing these literary cenotaphs and partly because Somerset Maugham had presented to Mr. Walpole a public reputation with which nothing much could be done.

It may be recalled that several years ago Mr. Maugham, in some such mood as that which led Miss Lizzie Borden to take up her little hatchet, produced a novel with the warm and cozy title of *Cakes and Ale*, in which Hugh

Walpole figured under the name of Alroy Kear. It was one of the most memorable literary dissections since Dickens' treatment of Leigh Hunt as Mr. Skimpole in *Bleak House*. Everything was there: the appealing charm that Walpole could lavish on those who were successful and might be useful, the bland indifference with which he could treat an old friend who had betrayed him by being neither, and—most unkind of all—his almost complete lack of talent. Maugham was at his best in describing just how Walpole overcame this (one would suppose) nearly insuperable obstacle to a literary career. His Alroy Kear, no artist with words, and with small powers of characterization and invention, made his own standing his work of art. He sent his early novels to all the leading writers of the day, with covering letters saying how much he admired their work, how little he thought of his own, and how much he would welcome their criticism and guidance. They were impressed by what they felt to be their discovery of a young man with modesty and with sense enough to respect his elders, and they responded by taking him seriously. They had him for lunch and for spacious Edwardian weekend house-parties. They gave him advice, which he took with an engaging, boyish enthusiasm and fetchingly tried to put into practice. No writer has ever been so affectionately sponsored by so many successful and established writers. There was, however, nothing snobbish about him; one did not have to have a great name to be useful to him. He was ready to correspond with the humblest reviewer. He was winningly grateful for praise, and it may be that his gratitude won him more praise. But it did not take praise to get him interested in a reviewer; he showed himself becomingly modest and eager in the face of hostile

criticism. His attacker would receive a letter saying that
the criticism was so just and so shrewd that he felt sure that
a friendly and frank talk with the critic would be bound
to help him remove some of the imperfections he knew to
be in his work. How about lunching together? At lunch,
he would be all charm, and the critic's reviews of his work
were thenceforward apt to be a great deal more understanding.

Maugham gracefully exposed the public-relations technique, which was all there was to Walpole as a writer, and
timed his exposure for the exact moment at which it would
do his victim most damage—when the resurrection and
mass reprinting of Trollope was showing up Walpole's
inadequacy even as a journeyman storyteller. (*The Cathe-
dral* is his best book, and its Archdeacon Brandon the best
he can do in the way of characterization, but the book is
only Trollope and water and the Archdeacon a thin ghost
of Bishop Proudie.) Not only that, but the older men of
letters on whose good will he depended, and for so much,
were dead or dying, and his contemporaries, such as
Maugham, were on to him. The young were interested in
newer and fresher approaches to writing, and the lending-
library and book-club publics—the backbone of his following—were developing grosser appetites than he could satisfy.
In the ordinary course of British literary events, this situation leads to a period of semi-retirement in which the writer
concerned produces a few essays with a golden autumnal
tone to them, opens bazaars, sits on cultural committees,
and marks time until the Crown at last honors him with a
knighthood or the Order of Merit and he reëmerges, on the
crest of a wave of Library Editions, Collected Works, and
cheap reprints, as a Grand Old Man of the English novel.

Maugham, with forty pages and fewer than twelve thousand well-chosen words, twitched this prospect away from Walpole and made what had seemed a certainty an absurdity. The knighthood arrived, in due season, but it was too late; Alroy Kear had simply extinguished Walpole as a serious literary figure. What repute he enjoyed at the end of his life he had as a bibliophile and, although he was notoriously foolish in buying fakes said to be by established masters, as an art collector who really liked pictures and who bought work by young painters and gave them encouragement and support when it was most needed. He lived out his last years, occasionally issuing odd, deflated novels with a curious streak of sadism in them, as a rapidly dimming figure widely known as "poor Hughie."

This reputation is not a negotiable one for a biographer, and Mr. Hart-Davis has followed the only possible course by reversing the normal procedure and exhibiting the less discreditable private personality in all its frailty. It is perhaps merely a coincidence that at the heart of the book, facing page 300, there is a portrait of Walpole by Walter Sickert, and that its frontispiece is a portrait by Augustus John. John's chalk drawing shows a strong-jawed, vigorously handsome man with something of a heroic and unflinching look; the Sickert portrait, almost painful in its pathos, shows a wide-open face, with a tremulous smile on the lips and a hurt, near-tears look about the eyes. It is the face of a solemn little girl who is always being left out of things because she does not quite dare to be bright and gay like the others. It is, as a matter of fact, this hurt little girl that the book is about; the John drawing merely shows the façade behind which she sheltered herself, her secret, gushing dreams, and her enthusiasms. One comes to know and

to understand this concealed personality quite well as Mr.
Hart-Davis quotes Walpole's journal, with its girlish excla-
mation points and italics:

. . . *what* a lot of books I have, *what* a lot of books I've
written, how much nonsense I've talked, how noisy I've been
and am, how good on the whole are my intentions, how muddled the performance! Have most people the sense, I wonder,
of being someone's unfinished knitting? And isn't it *very*
wrong to have so many things when millions of people are un-
employed and wretched?

Friendship with Virginia Woolf was exacting, since her
values necessarily challenged his, but stimulating:

My only trouble in my writing is that, wriggle as I may,
I'm definitely old-fashioned. Now I'd *like* to be modern. I'd
rather be a male Hugh Walpole to a female Virginia Woolf
than anything else on earth. How nice if they said "This new
novel of Hugh Walpole's *may* be very beautiful, but we can't
be sure because we don't understand a word of it. However,
we liked the passage about the silver snails and the moonlight
effects on the waterbeetles." I'd truly *love* that, and again and
again I'm tempted to do a little book anonymously just like
that. I believe I could. . . . I want to *prove* that my life's been
justified. It has if there's a secret life as well. But is there? I
increasingly believe there is, and from that all my happiness
comes. And *if* there is that secret happiness, it is based on Love
—no doubt of it. I love people more and more.

But loving and love are, alas, terribly difficult and set
about with pitfalls and misunderstandings:

Your saying [he wrote to Joseph Hergesheimer] that you
think of making a man's friendship your theme interests me
enormously. I could tell you many things about that. They

have been the finest things in my life simply because I've never yet found the right woman, but it's a dangerous and difficult subject simply because so many people will see it only as homosexual, which is the last thing it generally is.

Walpole had what was perhaps the misfortune to encounter two undoubtedly charming but somewhat formidable women when he was still an extremely raw and inexperienced young man. One summer while he was at Cambridge, he was employed as tutor to the nephew of Mrs. George Keppel, a great beauty who was at the time the mistress of King Edward VII. He came to know her well and in the end to admire her, but his admiration was oddly phrased: "Mrs. Keppel's great fun. I *do* like her. She's like a sergeant in the Guards with a sense of humour." A couple of years later, he was again employed as a tutor, this time to the children of Elizabeth Russell, a New Zealander, then married to a Prussian, the Graf Arnim, and living with him on his estates on the Baltic coast, which had been the scene of her most successful novel, *Elizabeth and Her German Garden*. The Gräfin thought him an attractive clod and tried to tease him—an activity at which she was one of the great artists—into grace. She was thirtynine and he was twenty-three, and she inspired in him at first a feeling of fear and dislike, which slowly changed to a deep affection that lasted the remainder of his life. The relationship was satisfactory in itself, but it probably did little to help him overcome the mistrust of women that made it so difficult—indeed, impossible—for him to find the right one.

The right man, the true friend, was also hard to find, though the problem was in this case selection rather than search. While he was schoolmastering, before he had launched out as a writer, he met a young Indian Army officer who was important, but not the complete thing. Then there was A. C. Benson, fatherly and protective, and then Henry James. This was perhaps it; he wrote in vast excitement to his mother:

It is a wonderful thing for me and will of course alter my whole life. He is, I think, a really great man. The honour is all the greater as Mrs. Prothero, wife of the editor of the Quarterly, told me yesterday that I am now supposed to have more influence over him than anyone, and say things to him that no one else can—and so I get given messages to *him* and act the diplomatist. He wants to come to tea at Lambeth and see all of you. I'm sure you would love him.

Quick on the heels of the establishment of this thrillingly rewarding friendship, another sprang up, with Robert Ross, who had been so close to Bosie and Oscar Wilde in the old days before the unpleasantness. The two friendships ran in double harness, and neither eclipsed the other. At Christmas in 1909, Walpole wrote to James, thanking him for the gift of five pounds, in terms that drew a memorable reply from the Master:

I am deeply moved by your word to the effect that you will "love me till you die"; it gives me so beautiful a guarantee of a certain measurable resistance to pure earthly extinction. Yes, I want that to happen.

This considerable triumph might have been laurel enough for an ordinary person to rest on, but it was Walpole's special gift to "love people more and more," and not many weeks later he met a young American, Arthur Fowler. A few days afterward, they were off together for a week in Lausanne. At the end of 1910, Walpole made the first of his annual lists of his special friends on the last page of the year's diary, a practice he kept up to the end of his life. The Indian Army officer was No. 1, Robert Ross came second, Fowler third, and then Henry James. The old man's rating did not improve, and when *Mr. Perrin and Mr. Trail* was published, in 1911, it was dedicated not to him, or the Army man, or Ross, or Fowler, but to "Punch," or Mr. Percy Anderson, "because you have more understanding and sympathy than anyone I have ever met." James wrote to his "dearest, dearest Hugh," teasing him a little about the dedication, and a coldness, happily not of long duration, fell upon the relationship.

It will be seen that the search was no simple matter of waiting on time and chance but was really in the nature of a quest ardently pursued. It was pursued in vain until Walpole was in his fortieth year, when (Mr. Hart-Davis does not enlighten us about the circumstances) he met Harold Cheevers, a London patrolman. He was a fine figure of a man, who had won many prizes as a swimmer and had been champion police revolver shot of the British Isles. The index summarizes the story of this deepening acquaintanceship with compact completeness:

CHEEVERS, HAROLD, history and description of 268-69; his character 269; H's plans for 270; H's trust in 273, 343; H's thought of 275; fourth on list of friends 275; enter's H's service 277; installed at Hampstead 284; in sole charge 286; fails to teach H to drive 292; as swimming instructor 292-93; H's growing affection for 293; *Rogue Herries* dedicated to 307; refuses to obey H 308; H gives power of attorney to 310; first on list of friends 311; unsusceptible to ghosts 320; becomes "hero of the islands" 326; and seat on Cat Bells 341; arrives in Hollywood 351; acts in a film 352; and H's picture-buying 354,

A page from Walpole's journal for 1940 is quoted on page 424; in it he remarks that he feels compelled to remain in London during the bombing, so that he can leave an immortal account of the sufferings of the city that will compare in historic importance with the Goncourt *Journals*. But:

This is detached cold and inhuman and mingled with stomach fear and a really terrible love for Harold and a few more. Why wish to be immortal at such a cost? . . . I look at my White Wall Utrillo, my Bellini, my Manet drawing, my Cézanne water-colours, with a burning protective love. Nothing must destroy you, I cry. No matter if I go—you must remain. They are certainly more important than I, but I would sacrifice the whole lot for Harold's little finger. Painters will paint plenty more.

Henry James's old friend had, one may conclude, found the real right thing at last.

This story, which would be remarkable even if it did not include a picture of the English literary world at a time when it was especially rich in personality, is told with tact and a feline discretion by Mr. Hart-Davis. It is a great deal more interesting than anything Walpole managed to write, and it altogether removes him from the shadow of Alroy Kear. He is revealed by his friendly biographer as a character infinitely more curious and more pathetic than that unworthy phantom.

George Orwell

[The publication of *Keep the Aspidistra Flying* in this country, twenty years after its first appearance in England, makes most of George Orwell's work available to American readers and provides the occasion for an urgently needed revaluation of it. The novel, which is his second, appeared in 1936, the year he said in his essay "Why I Write" was the critical one of his career, because he felt that during it he discovered what he had to do. This was to write political books designed "to push the world in a certain direction, to alter other people's idea of the kind of society that they should strive after." This throws some light, though not enough, on why *Keep the Aspidistra Flying* is what it is. Taken at its face value, it describes a man's fight to be a poet and a free spirit in a money-ridden society. He loses out because the whole weight of that society bears down on him with all its crass materialism and vulgarity.] He has no chance of happiness while he lives by poetic values; as long as he holds to them, he is denied love, creature comforts, and even, it appears, a chance to keep his neck clean:

The money-stink, everywhere the money-stink. He stole a glance at the Nancy. . . . The skin at the back of his neck was as silky-smooth as the inside of a shell. You can't have a skin like that under five hundred a year. A sort of charm he

164

had, a glamour, like all moneyed people. Money and charm; who shall separate them?

This passage has an obvious stylistic echo of D. H. Lawrence, but there is another echo behind that—of F. Scott Fitzgerald and his tormenting feeling that whatever a man was, and whatever he did, he could never capture the glow that emanated from the rich and marked them out as superior beings. In the passage from which I have just quoted, Orwell's hero, Gordon Comstock, looks across the bookshop where he works and sees the Nancy in exactly the same way that the narrator in *The Great Gatsby* sees Daisy, as a talisman that will reveal his own inadequacy. This echo sounds even more strongly in a passage in which Comstock is horrified to find not only that he has the tiny sum of fivepence halfpenny to last him from midweek to payday but that part of it is a threepenny bit. The discovery fires off a remarkable soliloquy:

Beastly useless thing! And bloody fool to have taken it! It had happened yesterday, when he was buying cigarettes. "Don't mind a threepenny bit, do you, sir?" the little bitch of a shopgirl had chirped. And of course he had let her give it him. "Oh no, not at all!" he had said—fool, bloody fool!

His heart sickened to think that he had only fivepence halfpenny in the world, threepence of which couldn't even be spent. Because how can you buy anything with a threepenny bit? It isn't a coin, it's the answer to a riddle. You look such a fool when you take it out of your pocket, *unless it's in among a whole handful of other coins.* "How much?" you say. "Threepence," the shopgirl says. And then you feel all round your pocket and fish out that absurd little thing, all by itself, sticking on the end of your finger like a tiddleywink. *The shopgirl sniffs. She spots immediately that it's your last three-*

pence in the world. You see her glance quickly at it—she's wondering whether there's a piece of Christmas pudding still sticking to it. And you stalk out with your nose in the air, *and can't ever go to that shop again.* No! We won't spend our Joey. Twopence halfpenny left—twopence halfpenny to last till Friday.

The phrases I have italicized show that this passage is really not about poverty at all but about the mood of a man who feels inadequate and despised because he is not rich. No such social stigma was ever attached to the Joey, the threepenny bit. When Orwell was writing, it was a small coin, the size and color of a dime, and the easiest one of all to lose. There was consequently a prejudice against it as intense as the dislike some Americans have for the two-dollar bill. But that was the limit of the prejudice. Comstock's feeling about shopgirls is as odd in its way as his feeling about the coin. Why should one be a bitch for giving it to him? And why should another one sense that it was his last coin, and despise him? It is the Scott Fitzgerald mania again, the belief that everybody can tell how rich a man is at a glance.

This feeling comes out into the open when Orwell describes Comstock's education:

Even at the third-rate schools to which Gordon was sent nearly all the boys were richer than himself. They soon found out his poverty, of course, and gave him hell because of it. Probably the greatest cruelty one can inflict on a child is to send it to school among children richer than itself. A child conscious of poverty will suffer snobbish agonies such as a grown-up person can scarcely even imagine.

What follows is another version of Orwell's harrowing essay called "Such, Such Were the Joys," which is a description of his own schooling at Crossgates. Subjectively, if one accepts this account of the process, it is a dreadful business: Two horrible people, animated entirely by the desire to make money and to better their social position, set out to break the spirit of a child and to turn it into a performing freak who will win scholarships when a whip cracks. Objectively, one can see the outline of something else. The school in question charged well-to-do parents high fees and used part of them to subsidize the education of promising boys whose parents couldn't afford to give them that kind of schooling. These subsidized boys were forced along to prepare them for scholarship examinations that would get them into the best schools in England, and they were forced hard because the competition was intense. What Orwell represents as an apparatus designed to cripple him was in actuality an attempt to give boys like him a chance to win the best possible start in life. Orwell's hatred of the forcing process, and of the exposure of his parents' financial inadequacy that it involved, was so fierce that he could never admit either the nature of the chance that was being offered or that he was, in fact, offered it. He proclaimed, instead, that he had been given a very bad education and had been maimed by middle-class snobbery. In a sense he had been, and the hurt child's feeling that money is the measure of all things—a notion derived from the experiences at school that are chronicled in "Such, Such Were the Joys"—is treated as the final truth about the adult world in both *Down and Out in Paris and London* and *Keep the Aspidistra Flying*. The two books have to be taken in parallel, because Gordon Comstock in the novel makes the trip to the squalors of Gorkyland that Orwell made in reality and that he describes in *Down and Out*. Gorky's knowledge of the lower depths was not a matter of tourism; he had no choice about making the exploration. But Orwell, a gifted man, with many friends who were anxious to help him, was never in the grip of real necessity. He sought poverty out in the hope that contact with it would, as he explains in *The Road to Wigan Pier* (1937), purge him of his sense of guilt. Comstock's wretchedness is voluntary, too; all the time he is suffering there is a good job waiting for him at an advertising agency. Orwell, in the following passage, explains the purpose of Comstock's visit in *Keep the Aspidistra Flying* with what seems greater candor than he brings to bear on his own behavior a year later:

He had finished for ever with that futile dream of being a "writer." After all, was not that too a species of ambition? He wanted to get away from all that, *below* all that. Down, down! Into the ghost kingdom, out of the reach of hope, out of the reach of fear! Under ground, under ground! That was where he wished to be.

Yet in a way it was not so easy. One night about nine he was lying on his bed, with the ragged counterpane over his feet, his hands under his head to keep them warm. The fire was out. The dust was thick on everything. The aspidistra had died a week ago and was withering upright in its pot. He slid a shoeless foot from under the counterpane, held it up and looked at it. His sock was full of holes—there were more holes than sock. So here he lay, Gordon Comstock, in a slum attic on a ragged bed, with his feet sticking out of his socks, with one and fourpence in the world, with three decades behind him and nothing, nothing accomplished! Surely *now* he was past redemption? Surely, try as they would, they couldn't prise him out of a hole like this? He had wanted to reach the mud—well, this was the mud, wasn't it?

The book goes on to explain that the device of degrading oneself to a point beneath criticism doesn't work, and ends up with the poet beating the system by cynically conforming to it and becoming a success as the advertising man he was clearly born to be. But Orwell writes this "happy" ending without much conviction; his mind is already warming to the idea of a universal smashup. It would destroy the middle class, which had invented the horrible educational machine that had hurt him, and it would destroy the whole world of money values, in which he felt himself inadequate. That Orwell's mind is taking this direction is indicated by a fantasy with which Comstock comforts himself in *Keep the Aspidistra Flying:*

Our civilization is dying. It *must* be dying. But it isn't going to die in its bed. Presently the aeroplanes are coming. Zoom—whizz—crash! The whole western world going up in a roar of high explosives. . . . In imagination he saw them coming now; squadron after squadron, innumerable, darkening the sky like clouds of gnats. With his tongue not quite against his teeth he made a buzzing, blue-bottle-on-the-window-pane sound to represent the humming of the aeroplanes. It was a sound which, at that moment, he ardently desired to hear.

This fantasy gets out of hand in Orwell's next novel, *Coming Up for Air*, in which it figures as a secondary theme. The first mention of bombing comes on page 19, and there is a prophecy of doom on page 24:

No guns firing, nobody chucking pineapples, nobody beating anybody else up with a rubber truncheon. If you come to think of it, in the whole of England at this moment there probably isn't a single bedroom window from which anyone's firing a machine-gun.

But how about five years from now? Or two years? Or one year?

This note is struck again and again throughout the book, and the passages that strike it take on an increasingly hysterical tone. At last an R.A.F. aircraft drops a bomb into the main street of the little town the hero is visiting in sentimental pursuit of his recollections of youthful happiness. (Needless to say, he finds everything changed, and for the worse.) The accident is described in a screaming fit:

But the lower rooms had caught the force of the explosion. There was a frightful smashed-up mess of bricks, plaster, chair-legs, bits of varnished dresser, rags of tablecloth, piles of broken plates and chunks of a scullery sink. A jar of marmalade had rolled across the floor, leaving a long streak of marmalade behind, and running side by side with it there was a ribbon of blood. But in among the broken crockery there was lying a leg. Just a leg, with the trouser still on it and a black boot with a Wood-Milne rubber heel. This was what the people were oo-ing and ah-ing at. . . .

I'll tell you what my stay in Lower Binfield had taught me, and it was this. *It's all going to happen.* All the things you've got at the back of your mind, the things you're terrified of, the things that you tell yourself are just a nightmare or only happen in foreign countries. The bombs, the food-queues, the rubber truncheons, the barbed wire, the colored shirts, the slogans, the enormous faces, the machine-guns squirting out of bedroom windows. It's all going to happen. I know it—at any rate, I knew it then. There's no escape. Fight against it if you like, or look the other way and pretend not to notice, or grab your spanner and rush out to do a bit of face-smashing along with the others. But there's no way out. It's just something that's got to happen. . . .

The bad times are coming, and the stream-lined men are coming too. What's coming afterwards I don't know, it hardly even interests me. I only know that if there's anything you care a curse about, better say good-bye to it now, because everything you've ever known is going down, down, into the muck, with the machine-guns rattling all the time.

There are two minor points of interest about this. One is that Lower Binfield, the place of remembered happiness in *Coming Up for Air*, is also the place, in the closing chapters of *Down and Out in Paris and London*, where Orwell is accepted by the tramps as one of their fraternity. The other point is the echo of the phrase "down, down, into the muck," from Comstock's reverie about his self-degradation in *Keep the Aspidistra Flying*. But the important one is that this passage, written in 1939, contains the entire substance of a novel written ten years later—*Nineteen Eighty-Four*. There is clearly something perverse in this. By then the squadrons of planes had done their worst, and Lower Binfield—which may be taken as a symbol for ordinary England—had not only known the dramatic, apocalyptic terror of concentrated bombing attacks but had experienced the mass impoverishment and long-drawn-out near-starvation that brings on revolutionary crises. The British declined to go to pieces under the strain; the big faces, the colored shirts, and the rubber truncheons never appeared, and no machine guns squirted out of bedroom windows. It would be unfair, perhaps, to say that Orwell was disappointed, but at any rate he felt cheated. Like a number of other writers who had thought themselves ill-used by prewar society and had been unconsciously looking forward to Armageddon and social shipwreck, he consoled himself by constructing a fantasy of universal ruin. *Nineteen Eighty-*

Four is not a rational attempt to imagine a probable future; it is an aggregate of "all the things you've got at the back of your mind, the things you're terrified of." Most of these, in *Nineteen Eighty-Four*, are of an infantile character, and they clearly derive from the experience described in "Such, Such Were the Joys." At Crossgates, women—the headmaster's wife and the "grim statuesque matron"—were particularly dangerous; they seemed to be spying on Orwell all the time, and whenever they caught him doing anything they handed him over to "the head" for physical punishment. This idea crops up early in *Nineteen Eighty-Four*:

Winston had disliked her from the very first moment of seeing her. He knew the reason. It was because of the atmosphere of hockey fields, and cold baths, and community hikes and general clean-mindedness which she managed to carry about with her. [This is, of course, the essence of the English private-school atmosphere.] He disliked nearly all women, and especially the young and pretty ones. It was always the women, and above all the young ones, who were the most bigoted adherents of the Party, the swallowers of slogans, the amateur spies and nosers out of unorthodoxy.

But the real horror of Crossgates is that the masters seem, by some kind of magical omniscience, to know what every boy does and even what he thinks. This horror appears in *Nineteen Eighty-Four*, and in the first fifteen hundred words:

The telescreen received and transmitted simultaneously. Any sound that Winston made, above the level of a very low whisper, would be picked up by it; moreover, so long as he remained within the field of vision which the metal plaque commanded, he could be seen as well as heard. There was of course no way of knowing whether you were being watched at any given moment. How often, or on what system, the Thought Police plugged in on any individual wire was guesswork. It was even conceivable that they watched everybody all the time.

The whole pattern of society shapes up along the lines of fear laid down in "Such, Such Were the Joys" until the final point of the dread summons to the headmaster's study for the inevitable beating. In *Nineteen Eighty-Four*, the study becomes Room 101 in the Ministry of Love, and the torturers correspond closely to the schoolmasters; in fact, they use some of the tricks Orwell complains of in his picture of Crossgates. Even the idea of Big Brother, which seems to be drawn from a rational examination of the propaganda technique of dictatorship, goes back to the same source. Big Brother, the feared dictator whom everyone pretends to love, is really Bingo, the headmaster's wife:

How difficult it is for a child to have any real independence of attitude could be seen in our attitude towards Bingo. I think it would be true to say that every boy in the school hated and feared her. Yet we all fawned on her in the most abject way, and the top layer of our feelings towards her was a sort of guilt-stricken loyalty. Bingo, although the discipline of the school depended more on her than on Sim [her husband], hardly pretended to dispense justice. She was frankly capricious. An act which might get you a caning one day, might next day be laughed off as a boyish prank, or even commended because it "showed you had guts." . . . Although my memories of Bingo are mostly hostile, I also remember considerable periods when I basked under her smiles, when she called me "old chap" and used my Christian name, and allowed me to frequent her private library, where I first made acquaintance

with *Vanity Fair*. . . . Whenever one had the chance to suck
up, one did suck up, and at the first smile one's hatred turned
into a sort of cringing love.

This passage from "Such, Such Were the Joys" does a
good deal to explain why the opening scene of *Nineteen
Eighty-Four* ends with the hero committing his hatred of
Big Brother to writing in his diary, and why the book ends,
when he has had his punishment in Room 101, with his
tearful declaration that "he loved Big Brother." In between,
the hero's spirit is broken by a man called O'Brien, in reality
his enemy, who pretends to be his friend and even lends
him a forbidden book he wants to read. As these parallels
fall into place, one after another, like the tumblers in a
combination lock, it is possible to see how Orwell's uncon-
scious mind was working. Whether he knew it or not, what
he did in *Nineteen Eighty-Four* was to send everybody
in England to an enormous Crossgates to be as miserable as
he had been.

There is another aspect of *Nineteen Eighty-Four* that
merits examination: In it, the bombing nightmares that
occur in *Keep the Aspidistra Flying* and *Coming Up for
Air* repeat themselves with manic violence and a general-
ized sadism that is clearly beyond control. They begin in
the first dozen pages, with an account of a newsreel in
which a child is mutilated, and they continue throughout
the book, alternating with even uglier fantasies about torture. The pretext is political realism, but it is hard not to
feel that what is involved is to a considerable extent a matter of rousing fear for fear's sake. The book is Gothic, in
the pejorative eighteenth-century sense of the word, in
that it seems to relish the murky and the horrible. But this

is not surprising; the mind behind the book is Gothic, and it reveals its characteristic pattern of distortion in the most astonishing contexts, sometimes in ways that are almost touching. While in Marrakech in 1939, Orwell feeds a gazelle:

Though it took the piece of bread I was holding out it obviously did not like me. It nibbled rapidly at the bread, then lowered its head and tried to butt me, then took another nibble and then butted again. Probably its idea was that if it could drive me away the bread would somehow remain hanging in mid-air.

Orwell cannot, or will not, remember that while they are sucklings the young of all such creatures butt their mothers as a signal to let down their milk, and form a habit that they tend to repeat when hand-fed with anything they like. Horses do it gently when you feed them sugar lumps. It is anything but a gesture of dislike. But then, there is nothing in the realm of common or uncommon experience that Orwell cannot stand on its head and interpret in a negative and essentially paranoid sense. There is another revelation of this warping in the first verse of the poem he wrote in 1935, and which he quotes in "Why I Write":

> A happy vicar I might have been
> Two hundred years ago,
> To preach upon eternal doom
> And watch my walnuts grow.

Vicars, as Christian ministers, are supposed to preach a gospel of love, and an offer of salvation, even now. The truth is that if Orwell had been a vicar two hundred years before he composed this verse, he would have been a Dean Swift, flinching from the same things with the same passion, and we would write of him as a French critic has written of Swift, "He carries the rational criticism of values to a point where it menaces and impairs the very reasons for living." We would also say of him, as the same critic has said of Swift, that "his personality is a problem which has not as yet disclosed the whole of its secret." Bad as Crossgates was, and bad as the state of the world was during Orwell's lifetime, neither justified a picture of a future order in which all children are treacherous and cruel, all women dangerous, and all men helpless unless cruel and conscienceless. Only the existence of a hidden wound can account for such a remorseless pessimism.

Reinhold Niebuhr

The Irony of American History comes from the pen of Dr. Reinhold Niebuhr, a liberal Protestant theologian. It appears to be a mildly critical essay on the moral attitudes behind our foreign policy, written from a Christian point of view, but it is in fact a veiled attack on some concepts that are essential to democratic ideas, the chief of them man's trust in reason. As it carries on its jacket a subtitle, "The Position of America in the World Community in the Light of Her History," it is clear that a good deal depends on what Dr. Niebuhr means by "history" and how he approaches its study. It is never very easy to find out precisely what he has in mind at any given moment, but he makes what is, for him, an unusually clear declaration on this particular subject:

Everything that is related in terms of simple rational coherence with the ideals of a culture or a nation will prove in the end to be a simple justification of its most cherished values. The God before whom "the nations are as a drop in the bucket and are counted as small dust in the balances" is known by faith and not by reason. The realm of mystery and meaning which encloses and finally makes sense out of the baffling configurations of history is not identical with any scheme of rational intelligibility. The faith which appropriates the meaning in the mystery inevitably involves an experience of repentance for the false meanings which the pride of nations and cultures introduces into the pattern. Such repentance is the true source of charity, and we are more desperately in need of genuine charity than of more technocratic skills.

The decencies of civilized social intercourse inhibit one from intruding on a man at his prayers, and this passage looks at first sight like a devotional exercise, if a disorderly one. On closer inspection, however, it turns out to be a statement of a purely secular idea on which the religious elements are hung like so much camouflage netting. The idea has been dismembered and its parts have been distributed through the second, third, and fourth sentences of the quotation, so it takes some finding. It is necessary to disregard the fact that the baffling configurations of history in the third sentence have become a pattern in the fourth; the odd thought that history is enclosed in a realm that in some way makes sense of it; the dramatic introduction of the repentance theme; and the drift into complete irrelevance in the closing sentence. What Dr. Niebuhr is saying, beneath it all, is that history can be understood in the light of faith and not in the light of reason.

This approach to the record of human experience is not a promising one, and when one discovers what Dr. Niebuhr's faith tells him about American history, one's suspicions of it are confirmed:

We were not only innocent a half century ago with the innocence of irresponsibility, but we had a religious version of our national destiny which interpreted the meaning of our nationhood as God's effort to make a new beginning in the history of mankind. Now we are immersed in worldwide responsibilities, and our weakness has grown into strength. Our culture knows little of the use and abuse of power, but we have to use power in global terms.

This is, if it is anything, a suggestion that fifty years ago the United States was not undertaking worldwide responsibilities involving the use of power. It was in 1902 that John Hay, as Secretary of State, issued a note reaffirming his earlier announcement to the great powers that the maintenance of the territorial integrity of China was a part of United States policy. The Philippine campaign in the Spanish war had been undertaken largely in order to secure Manila as a naval base, so that this China policy could be backed by a fleet capable of operating against the European fleets with Pacific bases. In 1900, a contingent of five thousand American troops was sent to Peking with the International Army that put down the Boxer rising, to demonstrate that the United States was vitally concerned with Chinese affairs and was prepared to defend her interests with force. Between 1899 and 1903, Hay, by diplomatic action, compelled the European powers to agree to abandon their efforts to break up and colonialize China and attempted to prevent Russia from occupying Manchuria. This so clearly established the fact that the United States was a power involved in world affairs that when the Algeciras Conference convened, in 1906, to discuss what were in effect purely European problems, realism led the Europeans to ask her to take part. It could be argued that this was a late development and that it leaves Dr. Niebuhr's contention that "our culture knows little of the use and abuse of power" unharmed. But if a rational rather than a mystic eye is turned toward such early American documents as *The Federalist* papers, it is obvious that their authors are very conscious of problems of power and that their approach to it is far from innocent. The arguments for the Union advanced in the first eleven papers all rest

on the desirability of developing a nation capable of equal-
ling or surpassing the military strength of the European
powers, and the fourth paper describes the instrument in
which federal power should be concentrated:

> We have heard much of the fleets of Britain, and the time
> may come, if we are wise, when the fleets of America may
> engage attention. . . . Leave America divided into thirteen or,
> if you please, into three or four independent governments—
> what armies could they raise and pay—what fleets could they
> ever hope to have?

It could be further argued that this paper was by Jay
and that it does not represent the main stream of American
thinking about power, that Jefferson's anti-foreign-en-
tanglement sentiments were the ruling ones. But Jefferson's
dislike of involving the United States in European conflicts
was governed by his opinion that they had their origins
in abuses of power by selfish interests, and his line of thinking shows a moral approach to problems of power rather
than an unawareness of them. And Jefferson used naval
power to enforce United States commercial policy in the
Mediterranean, showing that the innocent nation of Dr.
Niebuhr's theory was conscious of its strength and ready
to use it from the very beginning.

Dr. Niebuhr's intuitions about history appear to be as
unreliable on points of detail as they are on large questions,
and in his attack on Jefferson he represents him as the
victim of a particular fallacy:

> [His] conception of the innocency and virtue of the new
> nation was . . . expressed in his belief in the power of "na-
> ture's God" over the vicissitudes of history. In any event,
> nature's God had a very special purpose in founding this new

community. The purpose was to make a new beginning in a corrupt world.

But Jefferson said he was an Epicurean, and in his syllabus of the ideas of Epicurus as he understood them there is no God with power over the vicissitudes of history, or any place for any Being or Divinity likely to take an interest in shaping the domestic affairs of the Union. Epicurus advised a friend to "first of all believe that God is a being immortal and blessed . . . and do not assign to him anything alien to his immortality or ill suited to his blessedness." He stated that control of the physical and finite world of matter was one of the things incompatible with his immortality, and Jefferson commented on this by saying that the gods were not given to "meddling with the concerns of the scale of beings below them." The fallacy that God is an American patriot is in fact not Jefferson's, and the secret of Dr. Niebuhr's hostility to his thinking has to be sought elsewhere. The center of Epicurean ideas is the belief that by applying reason to sense perceptions man can discover what the whole nature of the universe is, can discover what his place in it is, and can order his affairs to achieve the maximum of human happiness. The center of Jefferson's Epicureanism is the belief that a rational approach to human affairs can secure peace and happiness for mankind. Dr. Niebuhr is in absolute opposition to this:

We know that recently the development of an inchoate world community requires that it acquire global political organs for the better integration of its life. But if we imagine that we can easily transmute this logic [of history] into historical reality we will prove ourselves blind to the limitations of man as creature of history. For the achievement of a constitutional world order is frustrated not merely by the opposition of a resolute foe who has his own conception of such an order. It is impeded also by the general limitation of man as creature. . . .

All these matters are understood intuitively by practical statesmen who know from experience that the mastery of historical destiny is a tortuous process in which powerful forces may be beguiled, deflected, and transmuted, but never simply annulled or defied. . . .

A nation with an inordinate degree of political power is doubly tempted to exceed the bounds of historical possibilities, if it is informed by an idealism which does not understand the limits of man's wisdom and volition in history.

Some phrases in this are danger signals—"man as creature of history," "historical destiny," "powerful forces may be beguiled." They show that a theological statement is being translated into the seedy language of politics. The religious dogma is that man cannot by the use of reason control or plan his future; his destiny is arranged for him by God, and it is sin for him to try to do it. The political implication here is that God is against such organizations as the United Nations and, indeed, against any major human effort. The irony of American history, as Dr. Niebuhr sees it, is that the material wealth of the republic and its successful exploitation have led Americans to believe that they can control their environment and their future, and that they have come to assume that their success in establishing their creature comforts is a sign of virtue and divine approval. It is his argument that Americans are in danger of committing the same sin as the Communists, whom they so much detest and to whom they feel so morally superior, since the essence of Communism is a belief that men can perfect a political mechanism for controlling their environment and their future. The concept behind this idea of sin is an old Protestant idea, which used to be more clearly and more effectively expressed. Thomas Burnet put it as well as anyone, at the end of the seventeenth century:

Man that comes into the world at the pleasure of another, and goes out by a hundred accidents; his birth and education generally determine his fate here, and neither of these are in his own power; his wit is as uncertain as his fortune; he hath not the moulding of his own brain, a knock on the head makes him a fool, and a little excess of passion or melancholy makes him worse, mad and frantic . . . with all these he is so vain as to think that all the rest of the world was made for his sake. . . . We are next the brutes that perish, by a sacrilegious attempt would make ourselves more considerable than the highest dignities. It is thought to have been the crime of Lucifer, who was thrown down from heaven to hell, that he affected an equality with the Almighty, and to affect to be next to the Almighty is a crime next that.

This is a clear and vigorous expression of what Dr. Niebuhr is saying in a more roundabout way, but if it is good writing, it is not very impressive thinking. If God created the vast expanses of the universe, those immense perspectives in the night sky that are so rich in possibilities of other lives beyond our imagination, it is strange to think of Him as a being capable of punishing men for hoping to organize life on one star in such a fashion that it is less disorderly, uncomfortable, and cruel. Dr. Niebuhr's intuitions about history suggest that He is such a being:

But the actions of those who are particularly wise or mighty or righteous fall under special condemnation. The builders of the Tower of Babel are scattered by a confusion of tongues because they sought to build a tower which would reach into the heavens. The possible destruction of a technical civilization, of which the "skyscraper" is a neat symbol, may become a modern analogue to the Tower of Babel.

Dr. Niebuhr goes on to talk of Babylon in this strain, and there can be no doubt about what he means. God laughs at human pretensions and brings them to nothing in a spirit which one would call savage and unkind if the relationship were that of a parent and child but which Dr. Niebuhr, since it is that of God and man, can call merciful.

This is a time dominated by fear, and Dr. Niebuhr seems to be expressing the scared reaction to the overconfidence of the last century. The economic unity of the world, which has created a community of interest between the nations, has been a reality for less than fifty years. Not many of its peoples are psychologically prepared to surrender parochial interests to world interests. They are not ready for the responsibilities and duties that they will have to undertake as members of the international community. They are afraid of the changes that living in an international commonwealth may inflict on national patterns of life. Dr. Niebuhr's defeatism seems to suggest that the effort to make such a world state is not worth making because the limitations of human nature foredoom the attempt to failure. His line of thought provides an excuse for not trying, and for evading the great new problems of government and equity that the idea of a world state presents. He offers moral justifications for taking the easy and timid way out. There is a certain irony in the fact that it should be even momentarily tolerable to Americans, who traditionally take such a confident view of the powers and capabilities of the reasoning human animal, that they should be tempted by doctrines that rate his potentialities so low at a time when their values are being challenged by those of Communism. The secret of the initial Communist appeal to the hungry, the rightless, and the dispossessed is its explicit confidence in their manhood and their powers; they are to revolt and take part in making a better future for themselves. Dr. Niebuhr calls Marxism a noxious creed on this account, but there are, one would think, other more convincing objections to it. What is, however, fairly clear is that his pallid pessimist declarations are unlikely to produce ideas that can be opposed to its dynamism. The rejection of reason, which is fundamental to them, and the lack of confidence in men that they express would seem likely to render those who accept them helpless in the face of any serious challenge the immediate future may present.

François Mauriac

François Mauriac, whose two short novels *The Weakling* and *The Enemy* have been issued in a single volume, is one of the intellectual pillars of the Roman Catholic Church in France. He has been called one of the greatest living writers by many reputable European critics who have judged his work by purely literary standards. His work is, however, primarily religious, and it seems to present a case in which the aesthetic approach is too limited. In 1948 he wrote a statement of his beliefs for a French magazine called *La Table Ronde*. This statement has now been published here as *The Stumbling Block*. It was interesting at the time not only as a profession of belief but as a singular revelation of the extent of M. Mauriac's dislike of women. He referred with violence to the cult of Mary and with contempt to those women who found delight in it. He spoke of the organizers of the innocent festivals in honor of Notre Dame du Grand Retour that were widely celebrated in France in 1947 as "pious Barnums," and of the processions and masses that honored the Virgin Mother as "this abasement, this humiliation of the Church." The vigorousness of his feeling was perhaps at its clearest in his remarkable gloss of verses twenty-one to thirty-five of the fifth chapter of St. Mark and the latter part of the eighth chapter of St. Luke. M. Mauriac had been speaking harshly

of those simple forms of worship that appeal to the naïve
and the illiterate, and calling them superstitions and manias:

> I was wrong to speak of vermin; it is necessary to enter into
> the charity the Church shows toward human frailty. The old
> woman who handles and caresses a plaster statue is the same
> who, nineteen centuries ago, seizing an advantage offered by
> the crowd, touched the mantle of the Lord without his know-
> ing it, that she might be healed. And the Lord said in annoy-
> ance: "Somebody hath touched me; for I perceive that virtue
> is gone out of me." Yet the poor woman was healed, all the
> same.

This was the woman who had had an issue of blood for
twelve years and had spent all her living on physicians, to
no purpose. Neither Mark nor Luke attributes any an-
noyance to Jesus on this occasion, and there is no flavor
of rebuke in the words He is said to have spoken to the
woman: "Daughter, be of good comfort, thy faith hath
made thee whole; go in peace." It is hard to feel that M.
Mauriac's interpolation adds to the story; rather, it changes
it, essentially and disagreeably. Since *The Stumbling Block*
was written, the dogma of the Assumption of the Virgin
Mary has been defined and promulgated, and M. Mauriac
has been compelled to add a preface recognizing the horrid
fact that a woman has been admitted to heaven. His recognition is not exactly graceful:

> I am anxious to state at the beginning of this book that the
> reserves inspired in me by certain excesses of the Marian cult
> do not imply any sort of resistance to the new dogma. . . .
> But I also think that the Assumption of the Virgin does not
> legitimize, any more than do her other privileges, the manifest
> abuses to which I am calling attention. On the contrary, it
> makes them more embarrassing, more dangerous.

Indeed, if M. Mauriac's observations are to be relied upon, women are dangerous creatures, especially if they are mothers. Paula de Cernès of *The Weakling* is no exception. She is a commoner from Bordeaux who marries into the provincial aristocracy to satisfy her craving for a title. But if marriage brings her the satisfaction of calling herself the Baronne Galéas de Cernès, it brings her little else. The Baron is hideous and sexually inadequate. He manages to give her a child who turns out to be a cartoon of himself, with knock-knees, skinny legs, a sagging, adenoidal mouth, and a drooling lower lip. After that he lets her alone. She becomes a monster consumed by fantasies of lust, and gives herself up to secret bouts of curaçao-drinking in her bedroom.

Before her inner eye visions arose beyond the power of language to express. Now and again she got to her feet to put another log upon the fire and fill her glass. Then she lay down again. The occasional flicker of a flame played on her face, revealing alternately the mask of a criminal or of a martyr.

The morning after this particular bout she decides to take the first step toward seducing the village schoolmaster. Her tactics are unsound, as M. Mauriac makes clear. She starts off in the rain, wearing a mackintosh, heavy shoes, and a beret pulled down over her eyes. "The rain beating on her face, she thought, would wash away the telltale signs of last night's orgy." Her exceptionally hairy cheeks are unpowdered, her unwashed hair is greasy, and she has not used any scent. "Looking as bedraggled as always, she set out to try her luck for the last time." The schoolmaster does not avail himself of the opportunity so generously offered him, and Paula turns on her wretched son in her frustration and fury and makes his life a burden and a misery. The Baron is moved to pity by the boy's sufferings:

Would he have to defend himself, at every moment of his life, against this woman who would be always there, the woman with the Gorgon's face blotched with bilious yellow? Hatred caught at his breath, but, more than hatred, shame, because it was he who had been that woman's torturer. Only once had he taken her in his arms, only once. She was, now, like a bitch confined—not for a few days only. Through all her youth it had gone on, and for years and years she would go howling for the absent male. . . . With what fantasies . . . what actions . . . had he, Galéas, cheated hunger. . . . Every night, yes, every night, and in the morning, too. . . . Such would be the lot of this abortion born of their one embrace.

Under the spell of this powerful and disagreeable soliloquy the Baron proceeds to drown himself and the boy. Paula soon after begins to die of a malignant tumor, in pain only partially alleviated by morphine, and haunted by regrets, but not for the man and boy she has destroyed.

It was of her own free will that she had consented to share the bed of a half-impotent monster. She had allowed him to take her in his arms, and that, in her eyes, was the crime for which there was no pardon.

This is curious, because it underlines the resemblance between *The Weakling*, which M. Mauriac finished in 1951, and his *A Kiss for the Leper*, which was published in 1922. The marriages described in the two books are identical, except that in the earlier novel the deformed husband was entirely impotent and the wife was physically attractive. The husband was, if anything, uglier than the Baron de Cernés:

He was so short that the low dressing mirror reflected his pinched little face, with its hollow cheeks and long, pointed nose. It was red in color, and seemed to have been worn away like a stick of barley sugar as the result of prolonged sucking.

Marriage was fatal to him, too, and it was knowledge of his inability to satisfy his wife's sensuality that made him wish to die. And yet, closely as the two books resemble each other, it is a difference between them that is in the end most remarkable. In *A Kiss for the Leper*, the impotent monster who has crept into the bed of a woman with normal and healthy desires is in the wrong; in *The Weakling* it is the woman who is in the wrong, and it is her desires that have become monstrous. This idea can be seen in development in *Woman of the Pharisees* (published in 1941), in which M. Mauriac handled his obsession with a good deal more subtlety; the desire for children by a woman married to an impotent husband leads her into an adultery that has a disastrous effect on her husband and her children. As usual, the satisfaction of the instinctive drive produces deadly results. In that case M. Mauriac felt a slight unease about the theme that has such a compulsive attraction for him, and after he had introduced it he addressed an unusual technical aside to the reader:

Subjects of this kind are, as a rule, instinctively avoided by the professional novelist, because he knows that many people find them repellent. . . . Renan once said that the truth may well be depressing. . . . On the level of human affairs it may be not only depressing but ridiculous and embarrassing—so much so that decency forbids us to put it into words. Hence the silence in which such things are usually shrouded.

M. Mauriac has certainly shown a rare determination to make himself heard in that particular zone of quiet.

Woman of the Pharisees deals with two abominable females, one a monster of false piety who disintegrates the lives of six people, the other a mother who destroys her son morally by spending a night at a country hotel with a gentleman to whom she happens not to be married. The affairs of this second woman present his obsession with the horror of feminine sexuality in another form:

There are many novels that bear, or might bear, the title: "A Woman's Heart"—more than one professional psychologist has plumbed the secrets of the feminine mind. . . . The man who was sharing tonight the Comtesse de Mirbel's bed at the Hotel Garbet lived for no other object than to reduce this mystery to its true and rather squalid proportions. His victims knew precisely what they might expect of him. Those whom he had possessed all bore about them the same indelible sign— the sign of a lust that could know no satisfaction. . . . One does not often meet a saint by the roadside, but neither does one often come across anyone capable of dragging from one's vitals that particular kind of groan, that cry expressing horror no less than delight, which becomes sharper as time lays its hand upon a body already threatened by decay, already undermined as much by desire as by age. . . . No one has ever written of the torment which old age brings to women of a certain type. In it they taste of Hell before death touches them.

Aside from what M. Mauriac discloses about himself in this preliminary generalization on the squalors of the feminine mind, one may detect a certain lip-smacking pleasure, an element of gloating, in the conclusion of this passage. And the statement that no one has ever written about it is not strictly true. M. Mauriac himself had pawed it over in

The Enemy, which was published in 1935. The central figure in this book is Fanny Barrett, a woman of considerable charm, who lives a life of frivolous grace—whatever M. Mauriac may say. She has the misfortune to be kind to a loutish young man from the Gironde, some years her junior, who has known and adored her since his boyhood. She initiates him into an international world of pleasure and of art, in which he meets musicians, poets, painters, ballet dancers, and choreographers. He is, however, irredeemable, and remains a self-centered clod. He treats her vilely, on the excuse that she has been tampering with his immortal soul, and after they have parted he goes into a decline, like a wronged Victorian heroine. She hears that her dear booby is ill and sends him flowers with a fond and forgiving note. M. Mauriac tells us, with approval, that his mother tears up the note, burns some of the flowers, and allows others to be trampled underfoot by a priest who has come to administer the last rites. The young man recovers, though, and is soon strong enough to tear up Fanny's letters himself. This is supposed to be a happy ending to the story, since he is by then determined to be unkind to Fanny but to pray for her soul. This is how M. Mauriac tells us that she has enjoyed life and kept her looks:

The modern miracle which has given to women the seeming boon of eternal youth produces in some people, of whom Fabien Dézaymeries was one, a sense of terror and disgust. . . . She looked as she had always looked, though the flood of time had swept her on, and each passing moment had marked her as with fire; five years of exigent desires and glutted senses, of lovers lost and lovers found, of passionate abandonments and bleak awakenings; five years of late nights, of endless cigarettes, of rich food, strong drink, narcotics, and drugs. Yet there she stood, her young body apparently untouched by the passing of the years, strong as steel, tempered and hardened and possessed. Sin, in its way, is a form of life. There is such a thing as *infernal* grace, and it can galvanize, just for as long as may be necessary, that adorable shape of moulded flesh which, according to St. Catherine of Siena, stinks in all its parts.

When one considers this rancor in relation to M. Mauriac's strained hatred for the poor Comtesse de Mirbel and for the abominable woman who gives her name to his *Thérèse*, and when one considers the peculiar vileness of the mother in his *Genetrix* and of Mme. Léonie Costadot in his *The Unknown Sea*, one must question the value of the whole body of M. Mauriac's often beautifully written work. It may be that a fundamental flaw is revealed by the uncontrolled violence of his feelings about those who like to burn candles in little bowls of ruby glass before statues of a clear-skinned young woman dressed in blue with stars about her and a child in her arms. Archeologists and classical scholars may inform us that the attributes of this member of the Christian family show that she is older than Christianity, and warn us that her cult appears to perpetuate that of the Roman Mother of the Gods and of the Great Mother who was worshipped before God became a man in ancient Greece. If this is so, her worshippers are, without knowing it, kneeling at the altars of Ge, who was the fruitful earth itself, or at those of Themis, who seems to have been the natural order. However that may be, the fact remains that the instinct to respect fertility and creativity that lies behind the cult in its primitive and simple forms is a profoundly healthy one. In turning his back on it, and expressing the loathing of the feminine principle that inspires almost every page of his writings, M. Mauriac seems to express a loathing of life itself. It is hard to see how writing, even though rich and elaborate, that is in favor of negation and sterility and that has, in the long run, nothing more to offer than a cry of protest against the nature of man's physical being can have any real value.

Graham Greene

The opening pages of Graham Greene's novel *The End of the Affair* are electrifying. They have a quality that, although it is hard to define with any precision, is immediately recognizable, the quality one becomes aware of as one reads the first few sentences of Henry James's *Portrait of a Lady* or hears the first few words of one of the plays of Ibsen's maturity. It informs one that what is to follow is to be an exhibition of an artist's complete control of content and technique. There is no falling off in the later pages of Greene's novel; it remains from first to last an almost faultless display of craftsmanship and a wonderfully assured statement of ideas. Greene has achieved artistic maturity, at once discovering exactly what he wants to say and the best possible way of saying it.

This arrival at a serene command of his medium and manner is unusually pleasant, since although Greene has always shown that he has had the powers of a major writer, his work has until now been torn apart by unresolved conflicts; his manner has warred with his material and his intentions seem to have been at outs with the implications of the actions he has described. The split was obvious from the beginning. In his first published work, a volume of poems that has become, as they say in the book collectors' catalogues, excessively rare, he describes himself playing Russian roulette with a loaded revolver. The action is appropriate to the stuffy indoor world of Dowson, and smacks of its pallid *fin-de-siècle* sensationalism, but it takes place outdoors—on Berkhamsted Common, a brisk, gorsy, suburban place infested with fox terriers and healthy children. The inner divisions are even more obvious in Greene's early novels, which are simultaneously loving tributes to Stevenson and Henry James and outrages against their ideas of what is permissible in the novel. Although Stevenson wrote *Dr. Jekyll and Mr. Hyde* and James *What Maisie Knew*, they united in putting off-limits signs at the entry to wide areas of human experience. When Hardy's *Tess of the D'Urbervilles* came out, James wrote an agonized letter to Stevenson complaining of Tess's animality and of the vileness of her world's sights and sounds, and the letter was sympathetically received. Greene seems to have made himself a master of their literary approach to life for the sole purpose of tackling what they most shrank from in it. It is as if he had set himself the task of finding out the sort of book *What Maisie Knew* would have become had James dared involve Maisie's innocence not only in awareness of the intellectual, non-physical tensions of her mother's relationships but also in the raw, tangible, and visible world in which those relationships were sexually consummated. For Greene, there were none of James's self-questioning aesthetic hesitations on the fringes of the problems of evil and pain; he plunged right into the murky halfworld dominated by the ugliness evil and pain create. He seemed to be doing for life what a certain kind of guide does for Paris, leading one away from its beauty and dignity to "the real Paris," a network of little alleys lined with curious places of entertainment. His researches into the nature of weakness and cruelty began to look, in *England*

Made Me and *This Gun for Hire*, not unlike a sadistic attack on the reader's sensibilities.

The religious element that first appeared in his work after
his conversion to the Roman Church only heightened its
sinister quality. Though *Brighton Rock*, *The Power and
the Glory*, and *The Heart of the Matter* were ostensibly
Catholic novels, as Mauriac's novels are Catholic novels, it
was hard to deduce from them that the principal feature
of the religion behind them was a universe dominated by
love and existing for it, or that a good part of its observ-
ance was a joyful celebration of the discovery of God's
love for man. One gathered that God's love was an uneasy
blessing that could be properly understood only by those
farthest from grace, and that it was not possible to know
good unless one was on cozy terms with evil. These three
novels are redolent not so much of orthodox conceptions
as of the addled Catholicism of Huysmans, who professed
belief in order to add thrilling ideas of sin and eternal
punishment to the inadequate qualms supplied by his sense
of guilt. In all three books the religious element can be
taken as simply so much décor pinned to questions of
sexual guilt. The actual pivot of *Brighton Rock*, despite all
the whoop-de-doo, is a comic and not a tragic one: Everything turns on the reluctance of its somewhat improbable
hero-villain, the teen-age leader of an adult mob, to lose
his virginity. Doom falls upon him when destiny has forced
him to accept the love of a woman and to lead her to the
marriage bed. *The Power and the Glory* is so much more
convincing as a story and so much larger in subject—resistance to intellectual tyranny—that it is easy to miss its basic
similarity to *Brighton Rock*. In it, too, the hero is undone
by contact with female flesh; he is destroyed morally and

physically because he has known a woman and she has borne him a child. It is impossible not to suspect that he had been made a priest in a church that requires its priests to be celibate merely so that his insane inability to come to terms with his physical and instinctive being will appear sane. The same issue is essential to *The Heart of the Matter*, in which a case of post-coital remorse is blown up until it achieves monstrous proportions. Once the hero of the book touches the body of the girl he loves, the whole fabric of his life disintegrates. Although he has been an incorruptible government servant all his life, just as soon as the taint of the flesh is on him, he begins to lie, falls into shady associations, is unable to refuse bribes, and slides down into corruption until he arrives at a point of wretchedness at which suicide seems a natural course.

Paying ardent lip service to the Church, the three novels bring remarkable creative power to inventing situations in which the Church is powerless to help and bound to condemn, in which its only function can be to define sin and to overwhelm the sinners with the knowledge that damnation is what they have chosen. Brushing aside the joyful declarations of the faith about the hidden manna that can fill the whole of life with sweetness, and its clear teaching about the possibilities of human happiness, these novels exploit with refined sadism the doctrine that the ultimate happiness is not attainable in the flesh, and announce that misery is inescapable. The clearer the vision of God, they seem to say, the greater the misery, because the more one becomes aware of God, the more obvious becomes the rottenness of man, and the wider the gulf dividing him from the divine. In Greene, as in Mauriac, it is possible to detect at the core of the declared belief a primitive fear rather than a creative faith. So far, his stories have all described the fall and never the redemption; in them, Eve gives the apple to Adam again and again, and he loses everything when he eats it. It is this fear of life and creativity taking the form of a fear of woman, so often found in religious writing, that makes religion repulsive to so many people, and a religious writer who expresses it does his cause doubtful service. In fact, until now Greene has allowed one to see behind his work only a faith that is an instrument of torture calculated to make any relationship between men and women, and life in the flesh, intolerable.

The End of the Affair shows another, happier face. The negative aspects of belief have gone into the discard, and with them the idea that weakness is the supreme power committing men to inevitable failure. At the beginning of the story, a writer named Maurice Bendrix, who is its narrator, meets the husband of a woman with whom he has had a meagre and disappointing affair. The husband arouses in Bendrix a fit of wild jealousy, because in a confidential moment of acute unhappiness he says that he has come to doubt his wife and is thinking of hiring a detective to watch her but cannot quite bring himself to do it. Bendrix, humiliated by the idea that she has found a more satisfactory lover, and wanting to hurt her and her husband with his knowledge, hires a detective himself and sets out to track her down. The four characters are the most fully conceived that Greene has yet invented, and their reality, and the reality of their situation, is astonishing. As the story develops, the bleakness and emptiness that surround them are slowly enlivened by a great wealth of feeling. The detective uncovers the poverty of the relationships that brought them together, but as he does so, the reader also becomes conscious of the extraordinary enrichment that has taken place. The woman has escaped from the mean and dingy world of self-seeking and has discovered the enormous realm of happiness that lies beyond it. The nature of the realm, as well as the difficult route to it, is described with brilliant certainty, and the effect of her experience on those around her is no less powerfully handled.

The narrator sets out, inspired by hatred and dislike, to discover a petty sexual wrong, and finds himself faced with a saint and a saint's knowledge of love. Saints have been crowding onto the literary scene lately, talking their heads off in the work of Mr. Eliot and mumbling dim intimations of an awareness of a greater something in Mr. Faulkner's, but none of them has done much to bring home the reality of mystical experience or the power that goes with it. Greene's saint does that, and the closing section of the book, which deals boldly with the miraculous, is one of the most convincing things that he, and perhaps any other modern writer, has written in attacking this problem. Where it approaches the effect, in particular, of discovering what she was and what she knew, upon the narrator himself, it is deeply moving. The book is undeniably a major work of art, and even those who cannot agree that the search for truth can be pursued in the neighborhood of the miraculous and the supernatural will find in it rich aesthetic satisfactions.

Denis Johnston

Nine Rivers from Jordan is an account by the Irish playwright Denis Johnston, done largely in prose, of his experiences as a member of the British Broadcasting Corporation's team of war correspondents with the Allied forces in northern Africa and in Europe during the Second World War. His assignment was to turn in reports that would be of special interest to British listeners and, while not departing from the truth, would hearten them in their struggle for liberty, freedom, order, and justice. The assignment had a special interest for Mr. Johnston, whose formative years were spent in his native land during the war of liberation and the subsequent troubles. Because he had seen the Black and Tans, the hoodlum force of irregulars the British had turned loose on the Irish population in the later phases of their defense of order and justice in Ireland, there was an enormous appeal to his appetite for irony in the assignment to accompany a British army on a crusade to deliver the world from Storm Troopers and S.S. men. He arrived in Cairo at a low point in the fortunes of the crusade, when the Russian front seemed to be giving way and the last major British fighting force, the Eighth Army, was being broken up in the desert by Rommel's Afrika Korps. At the first press conference he attended, the news of this resounding defeat was announced in Army language: "Developments in the battle have resulted in certain areas losing their former tactical importance. Accordingly, the garrison of Knightsbridge has assumed a mobile role." To Mr. Johnston's delight, the correspondents received the bad news not with cries of despair and dismay but with a burst of laughter. A theory of his was confirmed—the closer to action one gets, the more important one's style becomes, and one's behavior in victory or defeat becomes, even more important than victory or defeat itself. In this case, defeat was a fact; one should have been honest about it. The officer responsible for the communiqué had broken the rule by using Army language so close to the front, and the only possible reaction was laughter. A few days later, Mr. Johnston drove out into the desert to meet the beaten troops as they poured back toward the Nile valley in advance of the oncoming Germans. They, too, were not distressed; they were bored, and they were singing a battle hymn that emphasized their attitude:

> Oh they've shifted Father's grave to build a sew-er,
> They've shifted it regardless of expense.
> They've shifted his remains,
> Just to lay some bloody drains,
> To glorify some toff's new res-i-dence.

The attitude of troops, it might be pointed out at this juncture, rarely matches up to any novelist's concept of it. During the Battle of Britain, when Mr. Churchill was producing some of his most stirring rhetoric to enhance the civilian mood, a favorite servicemen's battle hymn was "Oh, why are we waiting?," endlessly repeated to the tune usually associated with "O come, all ye faithful." In fact, the only song of the Second World War that had equal appeal to English combatants and noncombatants was

"We'll hang out the washing on the Siegfried Line," but this one was sung very belligerently at home and quite ironically by the troops during the phony war and while the fighting was going in Germany's favor. As soon as there was any likelihood of actually beating the Germans, the British Army dropped this song.

As the retreat in Africa came to an end and a new position was stabilized at El Alamein, Mr. Johnston settled down pleasantly with the Eighth Army's fighting troops, savoring its curious pride, its professionalism, and its mixed feelings of repulsion and love for the desert by the sea. He describes, magically, the moment of joining this company of men. The battlefield is bleached by moonlight and the ugliness of smashed equipment is muffled in velvet shadow, the night wind stirs softly, and the beating of the sea on the beach is mingled with the growl of far-off gunfire. The talk, which has for some time been running on what good fellows the enemy are and how cleanly they fight, dies out, and at last someone says, "How about our bedtime song?" The radio comes on, and there it is, the song of the two opposing armies:

> *Aus dem stillen Raume, aus der Erde Grund*
> *Hebt mich wie im Traume dein verliebter Mund.*
> *Wenn sich die spaeten Nebel dreh'n*
> *Werd ich bei der Laterne steh'n*
> *Wie einst Lili Marlene,*
> *Wie einst Lili Marlene.*

It was in a sense a homecoming for Mr. Johnston, who had in 1931 written *The Moon in the Yellow River*, a play that deals mostly with the complex feelings for each other of the men who do the actual killing when great causes come to the point of conflict. In the play, the conflict is between Blake, an Irishman who fought the British during the rebellion because of his romantic belief in the kind of Ireland to which Yeats gave the most perfect expression, and Tausch, a German engineer whose romanticism is of another kind. Blake holds that the Irish can be happy only as long as they stay out of the modern world; the German holds that cheap electrical power and industralization will do the trick. The two dreams of a happy Ireland meet head on, and in the end they produce the same thing that war produces—the gunman who will decide which dream is to conquer. The irony of the play is savage. Lanigan, the gunman who arrives at the head of a detachment of troops when Tausch telephones a Free State barracks (Blake announces that he intends to dynamite the power plant Tausch is in charge of), turns out to have been a comrade of Blake's during the war of liberation. It was Blake's poetic love of freedom that provided the inspiration that made Lanigan a gunman, and the achievement of that freedom taught him that violence is the answer to the problem Blake now represents. To Tausch's inexpressible dismay, Lanigan shoots Blake out of hand. The subsequent argument, considerably abbreviated, between Lanigan and the German runs as follows:

TAUSCH: Did I ask you to commit a crime? You admit yourself that there is no excuse for what you have done. It is—I can use no other word—it is murder!

LANIGAN: Ah, never mind. I'm a physical force man born and bred in the movement. I'm only doing my job—the job I'm able to do, the job that always seems to deliver the goods. There's no excuse for it, I daresay. I don't pretend to be clever like he was. He [Blake] was the brains and inspiration of the movement in the old days against the British. But now we seem to have a damn sight too many brains, and inspiration always ends in trying to blow up something.

TAUSCH: And so you assassinate that inspiration!

LANIGAN: I suppose you think I enjoy that, when it means a bullet in my own back sooner or later. But enjoy it or not, I've always been taught that it's not words but deeds the country needs, and I'll have to go on doing what I can, no matter.

TAUSCH: A very fine attitude for young revolutionaries to adopt, maybe. But you are a man of responsibilities. The State cannot ignore the forms of justice.

LANIGAN: I don't know about that. It was he that always had the wit to find the word for these things. Not me. But I only hope that when my time comes I'll be plugged fair and clean like he was, with none of the tomfoolery of Law and Justice and the torment they call "Prepare to meet your God."

TAUSCH: That is all you have to say before I send this letter to the Attorney-General?

LANIGAN: Ah, what more is there to be said? I'm a gunman. I always was and I always will be. And if you ask me why, I declare to God I don't know. There's no glamour on my side, nowadays. But God help you all if I wasn't, is what I say. It may be brains and inspiration that makes the country at the start, but it's my help you're always telephoning for before the end.

For Mr. Johnston, the desert was simply a cleaner place than most, where the gunmen of two opposed orders could lay aside the humbug of the propaganda war and match their skill at killing in an atmosphere of honest mutual respect. When the tide began to flow against the Germans, it was the turn of the other set of decent fellows to retreat. Following the now victorious British, Mr. Johnston was

presently sitting in an abandoned German truck examining
the effects of a presumably dead German named Georg
Sichermann and reading a bundle of letters from a girl
named Anneliese Wendler. The girl, according to her
photograph, was any soldier's nice-looking, moderately
pretty girl, and the letters were any girl's letters to any
soldier. They came from Eckartsberga, a village in Thuringia, and Johnston decided that he would hang on to
them and return them to the sender if fortune should carry
him in that direction. It would be the decent thing to
do. Meanwhile, there was the perpetual comedy of war
to attend to, with its innumerable variations on its single
theme—the dissolution of private pretensions in the face
of its realities. He was, for a time, overwhelmed by the
powerful techniques General Montgomery used to impress
himself on the Army and the newspaper corps, and he
reached the point of recording his admiration for the way
the General had given the Eighth Army a new spirit of
confidence. But no sooner had Johnston done that than it
fell to his lot to accompany Montgomery's successor on
one of the self-advertising tours during which he handed
out cigarettes and other minor comforts to the men. The
new commander, rather awkwardly imitating Montgomery's democratic approach, paused for a ten-minute chat
with a truck driver. Mr. Johnston approached the honored
man as soon as the General had moved on:

"That must have been interesting for you?" I said in my
most inviting manner. "I suppose you know who that was?"
"Nao," he answered in his North Country accent. "There was
annuther maan wunse yews to coom roun' with cigarettes, but
ah think 'ee's gone naow."

The home-front myth of "the soldier's general" could not be more neatly deflated.

The road to victory led on, past many scenes of terror and a few scenes of great beauty, through Italy, through France, and into Germany. At every mile the innocence of the unpeopled desert receded further, and the moral confusions of victory increased. Now the gunmen and the civilians were all mixed up, and the high explosives and the napalm were falling impartially on innocent and guilty and friend and foe. It was all too clear that the fight to save civilization was doing civilization deadly damage, and the difference between one cause and the other seemed smaller and smaller. Mr. Johnston began a private war with those who had promulgated the no-fraternization rule, which he thought implied the communal guilt of the German people, and he put a great deal of ingenuity into a game with the censorship, in which he credited himself with a point every time he slipped through a report indicating that the German civilians were as decent as their fighting men and as uninvolved in the guilt of their leaders.

At last he arrived in Thuringia. He had long before lost Georg Sichermann's bundle of letters from Anneliese Wendler, but he remembered a phrase from one of them: "I had begun to think that you, unfaithful man, had forgotten Eckartsberga." Eckartsberga was not far away, and he turned aside in an effort to look up the girl. There was an odd atmosphere in the village, and nobody he questioned would admit ever having heard of Anneliese Wendler. At last an American officer suggested that he would find the girl if he tried a certain road out of the village. "Follow that road as far as you can, and you'll find all you

want to know." The advice was given with the entire con-
cealment of irony that is the one special gift of Americans
no European seems aware of. Johnston went bowling off
into the pinewoods with all his armor of cynicism and
skepticism shining, knowing that all the war's atrocity
stories were lies, that all causes, whatever their claims, are
naked self-interest, and that the only good man is the man
who is honest in the Elizabethan sense, as Lanigan was honest. And there, waiting for him among the pine trees, was
a gateway with *"Recht oder Unrecht—Mein Vaterland"*
written on it, and beyond it another gateway, more sinis-
terly inscribed *"Jedem das Seinem"* ("To each what is coming to him"), and beyond that were arrays of yellowed
and emaciated dead, stacked like cordwood beside the crem-
atorium, on whose end wall the jailers had inscribed a
final *gemütlich* sentiment: "Not a horrible and distasteful
worm will feed upon my corpse, but a clean fire will digest
it. I always loved warmth and light, therefore burn and
do not bury me."

Further on were hundreds of the living, squatting in the
open, dabbed with filth, in the throes of the acute dysen-
tery that was the beginning of the end in such places. And
beyond that was another place:

I went in. At one end lay a heap of smoking clothes among
which a few ghouls picked and searched—for what, God only
knows. As we entered the long hut the stench hit us in the face,
and a queer wailing came to our ears. Along both sides of the
shed was tier upon tier of what can only be described as
shelves. And lying on these, packed tightly side by side, like
knives and forks in a drawer, were living creatures—some of
them stirring, some of them stiff and silent, but all of them
skeletons, with the skin drawn tight over their bones, with

heads bulging and misshapen from emaciation, with burning eyes and sagging jaws. And as we came in, those with the strength to do so turned their heads and gazed at us; and from their lips came that thin, unearthly noise. . . . It was meant to be cheering. They were cheering the uniform that I wore.

Eckartsberga was just down the road from Buchenwald. It is a tribute to Denis Johnston that he is able to re-create the full weight of this appalling disclosure of the deep wound Germany had inflicted on herself and on the world. A Voltairian rationalist with a strong vein of sentiment, he had fought, as a great many other people had, against the knowledge that is an essential part of this discovery—"I did not want to believe such things of men, because they were not true of men as I had known them." Although he had seen Lanigan so clearly, he had not truly faced him, or the possibility that it might ultimately be the gunman's world. At Buchenwald it seemed to him that it was:

Appeals to reason were just a cover-up for this! Our good will has been used as a means to betray us, and that is as great a crime as the degradation of humanity, for it means that good will is a mistake—that destruction is our only means of preservation.

At this point, the book fails, since Mr. Johnston breaks into poetry to describe his recovery of sanity after the shock of Buchenwald and the sight of the naked horror the German regime had contrived, and what he has in mind tends to become obscure. One gathers that the guilt of victory descended on Mr. Johnston's head. In his rage, he picked up a pistol, although, as a correspondent, he was prohibited from carrying arms, and kept it until, in the final collapse, he encountered a captured high-ranking Nazi who had failed in an effort to escape from Italy through the Brenner Pass, and had merely wounded himself in an attempt at suicide. Mr. Johnston appears to have lent him the pistol so that he could make a second, and successful, attempt to release himself from whatever burdens he bore. It was an amoral impulse into which pity might easily have led anyone, and it is easy to see, too, that one might feel doubt about it afterward. But Mr. Johnston's doubt takes him a long way. The English edition of *Nine Rivers from Jordan* ends with a poem that is not in the American version. In this poem, man and God are confronted; God says, or A Voice says:

> Fight your own sins wherever you may find them.
> Outboast the vain, despise the proud,
> Neglect the slothful, and rage at the angry.
> These are your own transgressions
> And Pity is the Soldier's way to absolution.
> But, here is my command.
> Avenge all others' sins on me, as you have done this day,
> And leave the human race in peace.
> Come now. Tell me your name.

The reply is:

ACOLYTE

> My name is M or N and there is nothing to avenge.
> Here in my hand, I hold this creature—
> The fruit of the tree of my experience.
> Now, as the symbol of my maturity, I cast it forth
> And, like a child in the streets of Eckartsberga,
> I reject the inheritance of my father, Adam.
> (*He flings the gun away, and it goes spinning downwards from the altar.*)

OMNES

And this is my act of faith—
That I cast forth the Knowledge of Good and Evil,
And the deadly sins that are bred of sin,
Secure in the promise
That all things, future and past,
Hidden and revealed,
Are in His gracious hands.

As a private solution it has considerable appeal; it is a restful one, anyway. But what if one is confronted with another Lanigan whose gun is defending another Buchenwald? One is reminded of the meeting of the Irish rebel Michael Collins and another Irish poet, Æ, who spoke to him for some time in a lofty strain. When he had done, Collins whipped out a notebook and, with a pencil poised over a blank page, said, "Your point, Mr. Russell?" One feels that when, at Buchenwald, Mr. Johnston cries out "How did I ever doubt that there is not an absolute in good and evil?" he has a point that is filched from him by the incident in the Brenner Pass. When it comes right down to it, Lanigan can distinguish not only white but also a number of shades of gray from black. The fact that it was necessary even for the S.S. to write "Right or Wrong —My Fatherland" over the gates of Buchenwald is sufficient proof of that. The knowledge, for which Buchenwald is a compact symbol, that men can be dehumanized, and that they are capable of anything, is not a ground for casting out the knowledge of good and evil. That knowledge is the only defense there is against dehumanization and the essential basis of all rational action.

Ralph Ellison

Ralph Ellison's first novel, *Invisible Man*, is an exceptionally good book and in parts an extremely funny one. That is not to say that it is without defects, but since they are almost entirely confined to the intolerably arty prologue and epilogue, and to certain expressionist passages conveniently printed in italics, they can easily be skipped, and they should be, for they are trifling in comparison with its virtues. What gives it its strength is that it is about being colored in a white society and yet not a grievance book; it has not got the whine of a hard-luck story about it, and it has not got the blurting, incoherent quality of a statement made in anger. What gives it its character is a robust courage; it walks squarely up to color the way seventeenth-century writing walks up to mortality and death, to look it in the face as a part of the human situation that has to be lived with. Mr. Ellison's hero is a Negro of the South who starts out with the naïve illusion that what stands between him and the whites is a matter of education. He is given a scholarship to a Southern college that has been endowed by Northern philanthropists, and he goes to it in great delight, thinking that what he will learn there will pare away all his disabilities and disadvantages. He finds that the college cannot do that for him and does not even try to do it; it is concerned only with helping him make realistic adjustments to things as they are. He gets into a mess of trouble and is expelled. Before expelling him, the dean tells him just what the facts of colored life are:

"You have some vague notions about dignity. . . . You have some white folk backing you and you don't want to face them because nothing is worse for a black man than to be humiliated by white folk. I know all about that too. . . . But you'll get over it; it's foolish and expensive and a lot of dead weight. You let the white folk worry about pride and dignity—you learn where you are and get yourself power, influence, contacts with powerful and influential people—then stay in the dark and use it!" P.129

He is too young and too nobly stubborn to believe that this is the best that can be done with his life, and the rest of the book deals with his attempts to force the world to accept him on a pride-and-dignity basis, and with his final realization that he has to stay in the dark as an invisible man. This could easily be a glum and painful performance, but Mr. Ellison has the real satirical gift for handling ideas at the level of low comedy, and when he is most serious he is most funny. The technique is that of which *Candide* is the supreme example, but there is nothing archaic about the writing, which has an entirely contemporary vitality and a quite unexpected depth.

The first chapter is a little slow, but the second and third, which describe the trouble that leads to the hero's expulsion, convince one that Mr. Ellison is a writer with much more than promise. The hero is asked by the dean to drive one of the white Northern patrons of the college on a brief afternoon airing. By an unlucky chance, he takes the man past the house of the most notorious Negro no-good in the neighborhood, a man who is the embodiment of what Negro progressives call, and with hatred, field niggerism. The Northerner insists on stopping and talking to the monster, and a scene ensues that is an extraordinary piece of comic invention. Even when it is read over in a cold, analytical frame of mind and its purely entertaining aspects are set aside, it stands out as a startlingly good piece of writing. The monster's account of his misdeeds is in itself a tour de force—at once a brilliant parody of a kind of Southern genre writing about Negroes and an acute description of a psychopath's feeling about his actions, which includes, in a couple of sentences, a deadly cartoon of the relations between a genuine psychopathic criminal and members of the more optimistic schools of psychiatry. But excellent as that is, it is nothing to what Mr. Ellison makes the passage do on a more serious level. The student's reaction to the monster's story takes one deep into the feeling of one sort of Negro about another, but his reaction to the Northerner's reception of it takes one even further—into the heart of the very complex feeling between races. The Northerner's philanthropic interest in Negro education is a cover for a form of prurience, a voyeur's fascination. His real interest is in the Negro as an inferior kind of man, closer to the animal, more capable of letting drive on the lines of instinctive impulse and less restrained by civilized morality and patterns of conduct. Giving money to the college offers him a high-toned way of getting as close to these dark possibilities as he dares. It is easy to accuse Mr. Ellison of letting racial paranoia get out of hand in this particular character, and of producing an overdrawn caricature in consequence. But the attitude he is describing is a fairly common one, and is often given direct expression—

even by writers of great delicacy and sensibility—despite
its offensiveness. A poem called "The African," in the Literary Supplement of the London *Times* a while ago, put
it very flatly:

> . . . I fell to brooding
> On bronze-dark features facing me, the glazed
> Soft shine of jet-black eyes; on what a London
> His Congo-born, his secret vision gazed
> So gently, mournfully; beyond his waking
> Quiet behavior what still potent background
> Vast and primeval worked, what violence
> Ancestral under silences profound.

The poem, presumably toying with some symbolism about
a gracious innocence, went on to compare the man to swans
on a pond, but even so it is hard to think that it would be
pleasant to be on the receiving end of this sort of thing.
Mr. Ellison tries to show just what it is like to take it from
behind bronze-dark features, and does so remarkably well.

A good deal of the book is concerned with penetrating
to the unease and self-consciousness that underlie a great
many earnest white progressive approaches to The Question. After the student is kicked out of college, he goes
North to try to make his way in New York, and his adventures are told in a highly imaginative, picaresque story,
but, though the storytelling is excellent, in the end the
impressive thing is the analysis of attitudes that rises out
of each situation; there are always such sharpness of observation, such awareness of shades of feeling, at work. The
hero is caught up in what is clearly an agit-prop apparatus
of the Communist Party (Mr. Ellison does not, though,
give it that name) that is exploiting the color situation in
Harlem. He is a natural speaker and he is made use of in

campaigns as a front for the white committee. There is
not only perceptive writing about the feeling between
Negro and white in this part of the book but there is also
perhaps the best description of rank-and-file Communist
Party activity that has yet appeared in an American novel.
The endless committee discussions of tactics, and the post-
mortems after the hero's speeches, in which the nature and
extent of his departures from "correct" lines are thrashed
out, have an absolute authenticity. So has the picture of the
way in which the interplay of personalities inside the movement, and the constant intriguing to use the Party discipli-
nary machinery to advance one clique and set back another,
takes place. At last, the hero discerns the rank stink of
falsity in the Party line about color, partly through catch-
ing on to the way in which a white Comrade who has married a colored girl makes play with the fact to strengthen
his hand in policy discussions of district tactics, partly
through a realization that the white Comrades have used
him as a lure, as a Negro gull to gull other Negroes. He
sees that his district leader, Brother Jack, is just as much
Marse Jack as a field boss in a white-supremacy state. The
description of his disillusion with the Party, a true agon,
which is also his final understanding that there is no external
machine that can produce any ready-made solution either
to the color problem or to his own perplexities, is as moving and vivid a piece of writing on this difficult subject as
one could wish to read.

The book ends with a second tour de force, as successful
as the brilliant comedy scene in the Southern college town
that is, in effect, the book's starting point. The Party has
lost control of its agitation campaign as a result of what at
first seems to the hero to be a typical tactical blunder, and

the mass support that it has won drifts over to a straight
anti-Communist and anti-white agitator called Ras, whose
wild speeches bring on a wave of rioting and looting. The
drift into disorder and the spread of violence are astonish-
ingly well described in realistic terms, and through it all
Mr. Ellison never loses touch with his gift for comic invention. As the riot builds up, the hero realizes that not only
have the Communists an unfriendly interest in him but
that he is due for unpleasantness from Ras's strong-arm
men, who have him marked down as their enemy and a
tool of the whites. He disguises himself in bourgeois finery,
but the colored glasses and white hat he dons to put him
across the class frontier also turn him into the double of a
numbers racketeer called Rinehart, who is heavily involved
in quite enough trouble for two men. The hero's evasions
as all Harlem comes apart have a real nightmare humor.
And in the middle of it all, as the riot squads and the
mounted police move in and shooting begins, he suddenly sees what is happening. The Party has not made a
tactical blunder at all; it has deliberately surrendered its
mass following to Ras in order to provoke violence, so that
colored martyrs, shot down by the police, can be exploited
in the next phase of agitation in the district. The hero
emerges in his own identity to warn the innocents he has
helped to fool what is being done to them. But Mr. Ellison
has a tight grip on his satiric comedy, and he is not going
to let his buffoon hero escape into tragedy; martyrdom is
not to be *his* fate. A gang of white looters chase him up
a dark street, and he falls through an open manhole into a
coal cellar. The whites, enraged by this surprising vanish-
ing trick, slam the manhole cover down and leave him lying
there helpless while the riot burns itself out above.

Few writers can have made a more commanding first appearance. Up to a point, *Invisible Man* resembles Céline's *Death on the Installment Plan*. Its humor recalls the jokes that hang on Céline's fraudulent scientist, with his ascents in worn-out and patched balloons, his absurd magazine, and his system of electromagnetic plant culture, but Ellison's jokes are on the whole funnier, and his satire is much more convincing because there is clearly visible behind it—as there is not in Céline—a positive alternative to the evils he is attacking, the knowledge of a better way without which all satire becomes merely an empty scolding. It is a pity that Mr. Ellison's direct statement of the better way takes the form it does in the prologue and the epilogue, since they are the two worst pieces of writing. But the ideas toward which they fumble are as dignified as they are impressive, and it is perhaps unnecessary to have this direct statement, as they are so plainly implied in the rest of the book. It is not merely the Negro who has to realize that the only escape from the rattrap of worry about what one is or is not is to abandon the constant tease of self-consciousness. The Invisible Man of Mr. Ellison's title is the unattached man of Aldous Huxley's Perennial Philosophy, the man with courage to be utterly indifferent to himself and to his place in the world, the man who is alone free to be fully a man.

"It's Just Politics"

Edwin O'Connor's *The Last Hurrah* arrived festooned with pre-publication laurels. It was a Book-of-the-Month Club selection, it won the accolade of the *Reader's Digest*, and it was the Atlantic Prize Novel of 1955. In view of all this, one is tempted to raise one's hat silently to the cortege and to let it pass on its way to oblivion with the best possible grace. The temptation is all the greater because it is difficult to discuss the book without infringing on a number of taboos that can be indicated by saying that its main subjects are the nature of city government in the New England states of the Union, the role of the Irish in municipal politics, and the relations between city machines and the Catholic Church. The approach chosen is to bring two clean-cut young persons, Adam and Maeve (get it? *Innocents*), into this thorny area by having them taken under the wing of the boy's uncle, old Frank Skeffington, as he launches his campaign for reëlection to the mayoralty of a big Eastern-seaboard city. He loses the election, because he is an old-fashioned kind of political boss and times have changed, but in the course of his campaign Adam and Maeve discover what a charming, lovable, and heart-warming boss he is, what kindly, simple chaps—great-hearted, too, in their small way—his ward bosses and heelers are, and what a little thing peculation from the public funds really is, after all.

219

Adam sees the light at Knocko Minihan's wake, a simple festival made possible largely by the theft of a couple of hundred dollars' worth of food from a city hospital. In his naïvely priggish way, Adam finds this shocking, and he is also shocked to learn that most of the mourners are city employees drafted for attendance by their department heads. He confides his distaste to John Gorman, a ward boss and Frank Skeffington's only rival in lovability. "You have things a little twisty, if you don't mind me saying so," Gorman tells him, and then explains that Knocko has been lying in state for more than a day and that only thirty or so friends have come to see him. Skeffington is just trying to make the widow feel better by importing a few hundred of his own followers to give Knocko a proper sendoff. Having argued kindness to widows as a justification of theft, Gorman then puts the thing on a much higher spiritual plane. He points out to Adam that after the drafted mourners have had their stolen snacks and chatted about politics, the priest will come to say the Rosary and everyone will pray:

"I don't s'pose they'll all be praying away as holy as St. Francis, but you never know about a thing like that; maybe some of them will mean it, and maybe it'll do Knocko a bit of good. I have a suspicion that he's in no mood at the moment to throw away any prayers of friend or foe; he's likely to be needing anything in that line that comes his way."

Adam, falling for this use of the debating technique of shifting a position without appearing to do so, realizes that he has sadly misjudged the situation, and he is embarrassed:

He had come here tonight as the alien guest; once ashore, he had lost no time in the uninformed criticism of the customs of the land in which he found himself. He had been rude, and he had been told about it: it was as simple as that. Apologetically he said, "I'm sorry, Mr. Gorman. I'm afraid I'll have to plead stupidity and some pretty bad manners."

"Not at all," the old man said courteously.

While Adam is in this fancy and high-toned fashion becoming a consenting party to robbery of the public till, lovable old Frank is gently but firmly, in the manner of big-city bosses, pressing a thousand dollars on the widow to help her through her sad times. We gather that Frank is generous to a fault, and that he has not taken anything like as much from the city treasury as rumor says he has. What has stuck to his fingers has for the most part been brushed off in this kindly fashion. That his gifts have the obvious function of creating good will among voters whose favor can provide him with further opportunities for thievery apparently doesn't bother Adam, and apparently isn't meant to bother the reader.

The book's argument takes an interesting turn after the open admission that the kindly Mayor has abused the public trust and stolen public funds. A big businessman chucklingly recalls that a business meeting called by Skeffington and attended by the city's leading utility and banking men was enlivened by the following example of lovable Frank's wit: "We are united, gentlemen, in what is, when you come to think of it, a very considerable accomplishment. We've all managed to stay out of jail!" So from the starting thesis—that a kindly thief is better than a plain greedy one—the line of thought advances to the conclusion that because some businessmen have been dishonest there is in general no difference between businessmen and crooked politicians, that there is no great gulf between charging a

brokerage fee for handling a bond issue and slicing a little
fat off the city budget here and there where it won't hurt.
Mr. O'Connor's alleged big businessman remarks, "The distinction between private and corporate theft is a neat one."
It is not immediately clear why Mr. O'Connor is laboring
this puerile line of thought, and it can hardly be said that
it becomes clear as the story develops; what does become
clear is that the line of thought he advances is at once extremely simple and extremely confused. Lovable Frank's
principal opponent is Norman Cass, the city's most promi-
nent banker, and his means of opposition is persuading
other bankers not to make loans to the administration. Unfortunately, the banker has an idiot son, and lovable Frank
succeeds in inducing the young man to accept his verbal
offer of the post of fire commissioner and gets him to write
a letter of acceptance. This presents large opportunities
for making the idiot a public spectacle and for humiliating
the banker, so naturally the city gets a loan. When Cass
complains about the nature of the pressure that has been
brought on him, lovable Frank is instantly ready with a
comeback:

"It won't work, Mr. Cass," he said. "I realize I'm supposed to
redden with shame at the thought of playing dirty pool against
a distinguished opponent like yourself, but it somehow won't
work. I don't know why. Maybe it's because I just this moment happened to remember who it is who every year delivers
a bleak little statement about the pitiable plight of the people
in our slums, but whose own large property holdings in those
slums are shabby buildings not fit for dogs. Or maybe it's because I also remember that it's that very same man who engi-
neered the merger of the Consolidated Trust with the old
Mason Street Trust in such a way that one of his partners and

oldest friends was driven to suicide. I guess you could say that this man has quite a pool table of his own."

Mr. O'Connor is fairly explicit about what he is saying here. Cass is a representative of the old Puritan families that founded the city and made it wealthy, and that kept financial control of it after the great flood of immigration, drawn to this country by the growth of new enterprises, had broken their political control. Mr. O'Connor is saying that Cass and Skeffington differ only in that the first is a bigger hypocrite than the second, and that no distinction can be drawn between the traditional New England Puritan ethics of the one and the chiselling city-hall machine operator's outlook of the other. The point is made again later on when Cass runs a reform candidate against Skeffington; the reform candidate is as worthless as Skeffington, and his approach to the public is just as fraudulent. This is an irony that is not altogether unknown in American politics, and it would be a pleasing touch of satire were it not simply a part of Mr. O'Connor's consistent and unpleasing pattern. The journalist who does a series of articles exposing Skeffington's corruption is not only a hack who doesn't care one way or the other about the truth of the matter but—to judge by his language—a homosexual into the bargain. The owner of the newspaper that runs the articles is impelled by spite; years back, Skeffington's mother was caught stealing food from the kitchen when she was a cook for the publisher's family. He pretends to object to lovable Frank as a matter of principle, but the truth is that he can't bear to see his city governed by a man whose mother stole when she was a servant of his family. And so it goes. Skeffington loses the election, and dies soon after polling day, mourned intensely by his machine, a surprisingly small and compact body that has more affinities, in point of numbers and behavior, with the Ritz Brothers than with any big-city organization that comes to mind. At his funeral, a bewildering eulogy is delivered by a priest who seems to have known him personally very well and publicly not at all. A young monsignor asks the Cardinal to explain the eulogy, and His Eminence replies that he picked the priest in question because he did not want the public side of lovable Frank's career mentioned. This was because in the Cardinal's eyes Frank had committed a great and unforgivable crime in his public life—he had attempted to draw the Church into politics.

One can imagine a powerful and convincing novel written tough-mindedly around the idea that the old-time city boss was a rococo ornament to the political scene and the source of a barrel of rough fun, but Mr. O'Connor's sentimental presentation of that barbaric figure as a fairy godmother of widows and orphans is more than hard to take. It persuasively pretends that mean vices are virtues, and it is that rare thing, a genuinely subversive book.

Ivy Compton-Burnett

The big moment of *Mother and Son*, by Ivy Compton-Burnett, a British writer whose reputation is growing at a reckless pace, comes when an elderly gentleman named Julius Hume kills his wife, Miranda, by confessing to her that the supposed nephews and niece she has been bringing up in her home are not his brother's children at all but the fruits of an extramural enterprise of his own. He chooses to make this disclosure in the presence of Rosebery Hume, whom he presumes to be his legitimate son. The crisis of the scene runs as follows:

"What am I to say to you, Julius, in my last hour, on the brink of the grave? That I forgive you, my husband. What else can I say? What other word can pass lips so soon to be closed? And I say them fully. But I thank God that I have not dealt with you, as you have with me."

Miranda's voice ended on its hissing note. Her hands shook, and she pressed them on the arms of her chair. Her breath came shallow and rapid, and as her son approached, she suddenly threw up her arms, turned eyes on him with no sight in them, gave a long, deep sigh and was silent.

"Father, she is dead! She is gone from me, my mother! Why have you done it? Why did you think of yourself? Why could you not keep your secret? What did it matter, your personal burden, the weight on your own mind? Why did you put it on her in her weakness and age? It was for you to spare her, not to think of easing yourself. You have done an ill thing."

225

The gentlemen exchange stilted recriminations over the cooling body for a couple of minutes, and then a surprising revelation is offered; a Miss Hester Wolsey, the old lady's recently engaged companion, has been in the room through the whole thing. "Yes," she says, "I have been here all the time. I had not the chance to go." If it seems unlikely that Mr. Hume would not notice this comparative stranger before making his confession, it seems positively unnatural that she should remain immobile and inactive to the point of invisibility during her charge's seizure. The bare minimum of human feeling would require that she step forward to take the old woman's pulse to find out if she had merely fainted, had had a stroke, or was really *in extremis*. But we are not dealing with realities of human feeling; we are dealing with a heightened reality, or some such thing, so the companion pops up like a rabbit out of a hat when Miss Compton-Burnett needs her.

There is another remarkable passage, twenty-nine pages later, in which the facts of Rosebery Hume's parentage come to light. Rosebery, who keeps his mouth full of shriek marks the way an upholsterer keeps his mouth full of tacks, appears, white and shaken:

"Father! Let me call you that once more. I have no right to say the word. I am not your son, Father! Those are strange words to say. I shall have to face their truth. It is another breaking of my life. I said I had lost my mother and my father at one stroke. It is true in a sense I did not know."

"What is it? Put it into words," said Julius.

Responding to this rash challenge, Rosebery blurts out a hundred-and-sixty-word speech indicating that he has found a letter. "Let me read it to you," he says, with a truly

Gillettelike instinct for hogging the spotlight and the center of the stage, "that I may grasp the truth."

My Miranda, As you have always been wise, so you are wise now. It is time for the end between us. Anything else spells danger for you, and that is what must not be. The money is yours by deed of gift, so that nothing can arise to betray us. It must be for the boy in the end, but while you live it is yours. He can only live and die as your husband's son. Some wrong must be done, when wrong has once been done. The photograph you will keep or not, as you decide.

Yours to the end, though in silence,

RICHARD

There follow two and a half pages of discussion, during which the questions of the men's emotional relationship and property rights are polished off.

As silence fell, both men had a sense of another presence, and turned to find Hester at their side.

"So you have heard again, Miss Wolsey," said Julius.

"I could not help it. I was crossing the hall and could not pass you. I had no thought of your talking secrets here."

It is the argument of the many admirers of Miss Compton-Burnett that she is not dealing with the mechanistic realism that would lead any normal household to exhale this persistent eavesdropper with extreme rapidity; she deals with a larger wisdom that can be attained only by discarding humdrum superficialities. Thus, in place of plausible action leading to plausible developments of character, one gets a dialectical pillow fight in which people batter each other from one position to another with maxims of the La Rochefoucauld variety; that is to say, profound untruths stated with an air of authority:

"I never know why self-sacrifice is noble," said Miss Burke. "Why is it better to sacrifice oneself than someone else?"

"It is no better," said Hester, "and it is not really held to be."

"It does not seem that we ought to matter ourselves as much as other people," said Emma. "But I have never met a case of self-sacrifice."

"Thank you, Miss Greatheart," said Rosebery. "You do not regard my action in that light."

"It would be trying to be the object of it," said Hester.

"That would be the best thing to be," said Miss Burke. "There would be some compensation."

"Sacrifice should be anonymous, or it does not deserve the name."

"But then it would not be made," said Emma. "It would really deserve it."

"I wonder how it would feel to have a sacrifice made for one," said Miss Burke.

"Miss Burke, I fear it is an experience you have not met," said Rosebery.

"Have you met it?" said Julius.

"I remember many instances of it in my mother's dealings with me."

"They should hardly count. They would have satisfied herself."

And so on and on. One breath of the realities of relationships between men and women would disintegrate the whole fabric and reveal the poverty not only of the observation behind the dialogue but also of the intellectual process. Even if it is held that the author is making a flank march on coldness and selfishness, a liberal view that the text does nothing to support, the dialogue still falls apart, since the cold and selfish know better than anyone else, it being the source of their emotional daily bread, how

common self-sacrifice is. This typical exchange is in fact
the brisk rattle of small talk, noise that fills up the vacuum
created by a determination to say nothing important. A
convention of tart unmannerliness creates an atmosphere
of candor which conceals the fact that all damaging holds
are barred:

> "You are not as simple as you pretend to be."
> "Oh, no, dear. It is the form my cleverness takes."
> "You mean it is the form you give it."

These cozy thrusts will never slip between the ribs into
the lungs; the weapons are not rapiers but buttoned foils
that will bend double against a jacket and at most produce
a murmur of "*Touché*." It is a matter not of wit but of
mechanical fooling, and despite the air of utter frankness,
no harm is done. What one is face to face with is not the
devastating insight into human relationships that should
spring from events of the order of the death scene and the
discovery of paternity which are the core of this book but
the mildest conventions of an almost repulsively parochial
society dressed up to look like courageous explorations.
That is perhaps the secret of the current British vogue for
Miss Compton-Burnett's work; it has an air of being utterly
ruthless, but it leaves everything disturbing and challenging severely alone. The vogue for this sort of thing was
established by the nostalgic resurrection of Henry James
as a great reputation. James's visions of country-house
England, and his pictures of English and French life, meant
very little when they were new because they were manifestly at variance with the experiences of his contemporaries. They began to acquire validity of a kind after the
First World War, when the horrors of the new order lent

a pleasant glow to the Edwardian period. The dingy 'twenties, with their steady erosions of private life by threatening political and economic events, were succeeded by the decades of misery when mass movements and mass events, such as the depression, took complete charge of private life, and the Jamesian heyday became a golden age to be looked back on with intense longing, the longing with which Talleyrand and other men of his generation looked back on the last years of the *ancien régime*. The Master's novels gave a picture of life before the Flood, when people could concentrate on their own affairs in the warm sunlight of a stable and happy world that existed only as a background. It is worth noting that James's rise in esteem corresponds almost exactly with the fall in esteem of the Edwardian writers whose work gives, in setting and background, an authentic picture of their far from ideal times and also with the development of a theory that setting and background are unimportant accessories of the drama of relationships.

Miss Compton-Burnett has in her novels evolved a stylistic trick that exploits this conception to the logical end. The background is almost entirely eliminated, as scenery was in certain avant-garde theatrical productions of thirty years ago, and what little exists emerges only by implication from the dialogue. The language—one never spoken by any human race before or since the Flood—announces that one is faced with a period piece, and a ticket at the corner of the bare stage announces that the year is 1897. Its detail is up to the reader, and he can construct it in accordance with his own fantasies and so exempt himself from the harsh realities of his own times—if there had been no horrid wars, if his parents had not had to give up their comfortable old Georgian house (now the local telephone exchange), if servants were still easy to get, if incomes had kept their value and taxes had stayed at a reasonable level, he, too, might be living in one of the teeming three-genera-tion family warrens that Miss Compton-Burnett describes again and again. Her novels are, however, realistic in the sense that they are not for those who go climbing socially in their fantasies; unlike those of Henry James, which cater to readers who prefer to transport themselves up the social ladder in their daydreams, they picture the ideal world of those who will admit to being middle-class. But basically this kind of fiction functions exactly on the level of the lighter kind of historical novel, taking the reader out of his own epoch and transporting him to whatever he sees as his particular golden age—the "stap-me, Sir Harry" eight-eenth century, or the Good King Charles merrie seven-teenth, of the franker purveyors of dream stuff. The dreams, though, are milder, being concerned not with swashbuckling or womanizing but with such refinements as having plenty of maids in aprons on hand to do the dirty work. Their flavor is exquisitely conveyed by the opening sentence of James's *Portrait of a Lady:* "Under certain circumstances there are few hours in life more agreeable than the hour dedicated to the ceremony known as after-noon tea." The remark sets the tone of artistic seriousness in which the question of whether or not Lord Warburton or Caspar Goodwood will succeed in arousing the passions of sexually timid Isabel Archer is explored for four hundred and thirty pages. It is rather a comedown from Lord War-burton, with his hundred thousand a year, his seat in Par-liament, his half-dozen houses, and his fifty thousand acres, to poor Julius Hume and his bourgeois ambiance, but they at least inhabit the same spiritual realm. One may recall the delicacy and restraint with which Mr. Hume's wife, the mother of *Mother and Son*, died: she "gave a long, deep sigh and was silent." Death is after all a little thing that stops one character talking and gives a new turn to the talk of the others; such are the values of afternoon-tea letters.

The Greek Myth

Mr. Robert Graves, the poet who recently reëxamined the New Testament and presented us with the definitive text of a lost gospel restored on the basis of his own poetic intuitions, has now rewritten all the legends of the gods and heroes of Hellas in *The Greek Myths*. He is perhaps the only living man whose stature and breadth of knowledge justify embarking on such enterprises, and whose ability as a writer is great enough to take them out of the realm of arid theorizing and into the realm of aesthetic pleasure. The publication of the two volumes to which this magisterial, disturbing, and altogether fascinating work runs is a little untimely; it is a few years too late for the centenary of Hawthorne's *Wonder Book* and *Tanglewood Tales* and it is a year too early to celebrate the four-hundredth anniversary of the appearance of Vincenzo Cartari's *Images of the Gods*. Cartari's book was the first popular mythology of the Renaissance, for although other mythographers had brought out studies of the old gods before 1556, he was the first to write not in Latin but in the vulgar tongue, for the general public. This gives his study an affinity with Mr. Graves', which makes its appearance at ninety-five cents a volume and in the pocket-book format of the Penguin Library. At least one other affinity comes to mind. Modern scholars squalidly devoted to specialization avert their eyes when Mr. Graves makes his Hussar rides through their neatly tended pastures on the winged horse of his intuitions; scholars of Cartari's day rarely mentioned his book, although it became a best-seller, running through twelve Italian, one English, one German, five Latin, and five French editions. One of the few scholars who ever referred to it was Robert Burton, who knew it under its pleasing English title of *The Fountain of Ancient Fiction* and was appalled by it. He was so disagreeably impressed by the illustrations, showing Jupiter with a ram's head, Mercury with a dog's head, Pan as a goat, and Hecate with three heads—an ass, a pig, and a dog—that he was led to classify mythology as yet another manifestation of the disease of the imagination that he called melancholy.

Burton's reaction was not in the least perverse or eccentric, since in his time the old gods had reached the nadir of their Christian-era misfortunes. When the new religion banished them from their temples, they still possessed what appeared to be one secure stronghold. For centuries before they were challenged by Christianity, they had been quietly consolidating their hold on the heavenly bodies and the constellations, and their names had become unshakably attached to the stars of the night sky and the planets. This stronghold proved to be a trap, and the humbled gods were involved in a long sequence of misadventures, which Jean Seznec has entertainingly described in *Survival of the Pagan Gods*. Christianity, he points out, turned its back on the natural sciences, and the study of the stars fell into disrepute. Astronomy, which had come west from the Chaldeans to the Greeks, returned east, to be taken up by the Arabs. They adopted the names that appeared on the Greek sky charts, and followed the established practice of enclosing the diagrams of the various constellations within drawings of the gods and heroes from whom they took their names, and the Arab draftsmen naturally put them into Oriental dress; thus Hercules acquired a turban, Mercury's winged hat became a coxcomb. The blood dripping from the head of Medusa carried by Perseus was misconstrued to be the red beard of a male demon. When astronomy reëntered the Christian world by the back door, as astrology, to be taken up by the semi-literate horde of fortune-tellers and charlatans who were the heirs to the classical sciences, the gods underwent still more surprising transformations. Mars in his chariot, flogging on his horses with a whip, became a medieval knight riding in a farm cart and carrying a flail for threshing corn. This was because a translator replaced the Latin word *"flagellum,"* meaning "whip," with the French word *"flayeu,"* meaning "flail." The enigmatic figure created by this confusion then acquired his own legend, and, as the Knight in the Cart in the Arthurian romances, Mars ended his journey from Olympus in complete anonymity. The gods also found themselves, inextricably confused with lower-class demons from Egypt and Assyria and dressed like mountebanks, turning up in the fortune-tellers' booths on the greasy cards of the *tarocco*, or tarot, pack.

It was from this fate that Cartari, in his *Images of the Gods*, set out to rescue them. His purpose was, quite simply, to stabilize the iconography of Olympus and to restore the gods and heroes to their original shapes. His methods were naïve, and they make one realize that he was operating in the infancy of the science of paleography. He considered all documents of equal value, regardless of their date or of the corruption of their texts, and reassembled his Olympians from whatever descriptions he could find. His authorities were the Latin classics of pagan times, Early Christian polemics against the old religion, and even the fantasies of magicians like Hermes Trismegistus. His gods, in consequence, seemed wholly bizarre to Burton, and essentially barbaric. They were, in a word, quite unsuitable as the presiding deities of the new humanism of the Renaissance, which had already determined to invest them with entirely different characteristics.

A fascinating study of the history of ideas is afforded by a study of the treatment of mythological themes in any well-illustrated history of art. As the ideology of the new humanism becomes the dominant element in European culture, the gods rapidly gain in respectability, and even before the first half century of the High Renaissance has run its course any representation of the Olympians consists of a grouping of well-tubbed members of the upper classes. Their tendency to plumpness shows that they live without occasion for exertion, and there are other evidences that they are extremely well-to-do. Their clothing, always in appetizing disarray, is made of the finest materials, and the massive gem-encrusted jewelry of the goddesses is of imperial splendor. In a single century, the gods move from the fortune-tellers' booths to the palaces of the aristocrats and become aristocrats themselves. In a vault of the Tour de la Ligue, in the Burgundian château of Tanlay, a pretty compliment is paid by the Coligny-Châtillon family to Henri II of France, who appears there as Jupiter. The Duchess of Ferrara is close by as Themis, the Connétable de Montmorency as Mars, and the Cardinal of Lorraine as Mercury. Mythology has at this point become political, and the Olympians have become the totems of the new absolutist state. The way is open for the apotheosis of Louis XIV, who is represented in image and language throughout his reign as Phoebus Apollo, the Sun King, and the myths take on the aspect of the scandals of an opulent court.

In view of the political developments of the eighteenth century, as the rise of the middle class and the ideas of liberalism prepared the way for the great bourgeois triumph of the nineteenth, one would expect a new expulsion from Olympus. The fall of the Bastille should have sent the gods begging again, to live in exile like the adherents of the *ancien régime* they had become. But they had learned to be pliant and foresighted in their years of hardship. They had allied only their Roman personalities to absolutism, and when the hour of bourgeois triumph struck, they were ready to reverse all their alliances under cover of the Greek Revival.

The intellectual comedy went forward smoothly and gracefully from the start, when the first scholarly visit to the ruins of Athens was made by James ("Athenian") Stuart, the British architect, painter, and author, in 1751. Within twenty-five years, the brand-new (to European eyes) image of the Acropolis and the Parthenon had been impressed on the Western mind as the symbol of the city of free men and free thought. The Olympians underwent a complete change, dropping their Roman names and reforming all their habits. The rich brocades and wispy muslins of their absolutist days gave way to plain white woollens, the gods became sun-tanned and athletic, and every goddess and nymph took off twenty to forty pounds. Their ornate jewels were replaced by severe goldsmith's work, and the baroque glory of their heavenly mansions was abandoned for the chastity of white marble. There was an almost Quaker simplicity about their underfurnished apartments. By the time of Louis Philippe, the Citizen King, the gods had become hard-working bourgeois whose lives were devoted to the discharge of the heavy responsibilities their rise to a leading position in the community had brought them.

An ideal Greece was invented to conform with the new liberal, democratic iconography. One can see it in its refined perfection in the imaginary landscapes of the great German Grecian architect Karl Friedrich Schinkel, who at one time planned to plane off the top of the Acropolis and erect upon it a palace for the King of Greece that would in effect be a kind of temple to Athene, Goddess of Constitutional Monarchy. One of his canvases shows a temple under construction. There are no ill-fed proletarians in sight. The work is being done by superbly muscled athletes who clearly consider their noble task a rewarding form of sport. Behind them is a wide landscape, Greek in its nobility and South German in its *gemütlich* softness and generosity. Lovely buildings rise on every side among splendid trees, and wherever there is a break in the woodland there is a stretch of lawnlike pasture. It is the vision of Greece that Keats expressed in "Ode on a Grecian Urn," and it recalls every cliché in the antiquarian repertory—the shepherds piping, the light-footed girls bringing in the harvest with a choral dance, the flower-decked heifers, and the nymphs of the groves.

This dreaming had its eminently practical side; the visionary landscapes included poets who magically anticipated the nineteenth-century ethos. When Hesiod and Homer met, they exchanged (so says Hesiod) views any Victorian schoolmaster could endorse:

HESIOD:

What is the best thing of all for a man to ask of the Gods
in prayer?

HOMER:

That he may be always at peace with himself continually.

HESIOD:

Can you tell me in briefest space what is best of all?

HOMER:

A sound mind in a manly body, as I believe.

HESIOD:

Of what effect are righteousness and courage?

HOMER:

To advance the common good by private pains.

HESIOD:

What is the mark of wisdom among men?

HOMER:

To read aright the present, and to march with the occasion.

Hesiod, a Jeffersonian character who was a combination
of unsuccessful farmer and inspirational public figure, not
only catered to the Sunday-go-to-meeting aspects of bourgeois morality but also provided for its weekday and more
robust side by writing the earliest known invocation to
what has been variously called Competition, Free Enterprise, and Beneficent Strife:

The elder daughter of dark Night . . . she stirs up even the
shiftless to toil; for a man grows eager to work when he considers his neighbor, a rich man who hastens to plough and
plant and put his house in good order, and neighbor vies with
his neighbor as he hurries after wealth. This Strife is whole-
some for men.

It is not surprising that complete self-identification with such right-minded people was easy for the new masters of society, or that banks were often built in the shape of Greek temples, nor is it surprising that the three countries in which the Greek Revival enjoyed its most sweeping successes were France, Germany, and the United States. In the first two of these countries, Greek history and the Greek cultural heritage served as perfect substitutes for a past that was being repudiated, and in the last they served for one that had never existed. In Germany and in America, there was the additional link of the federal idea. The alliances between the city-states of Greece, cemented by common religious faiths and political ideals, offered a pleasing analogy with the American alliance of sovereign states and the newly unified Greater Germany. Strong as the appeal of Republican Rome still was, Rome was tainted with the idea of Caesarism and with the concept of the monolithic centralized imperial government that took over from the Senate. Greece was the spiritual homeland, and its gods were guardians of the liberal, democratic civic tradition. Its history had shortcomings, but Victorian historians courageously dealt with some of these by filling in gaps and making discreet amplifications. Plutarch, for instance, was fairly frank in admitting that, six hundred years after Solon's death, he knew very little about the celebrated reformer, but Bury, the English historian, writing eighteen hundred years later, even knew how he thought:

The social abuses and the sad state of the masses were clear to everybody, but Solon saw another side of the question; and he had no sympathy with the extreme revolutionary agitators who demanded a redistribution of lands.

While this fabrication of a historical middle-class Greece was going on, mythology was also being reformed. The new approach is exemplified to perfection by Hawthorne in *A Wonder Book* and *Tanglewood Tales*. In his version of the story of the Minotaur, Theseus's mother (whose troubles stemmed from her having slept with Poseidon and Aegeus, who was drunk at the time, on the same night) is the epitome of suburban decency when she explains to her nice little boy why Daddy never comes to see them now:

Theseus was very fond of hearing about King Aegeus, and often asked his good mother Aethra why he did not come and live with them at Troezene.

"Ah my dear son," answered Aethra, with a sigh, "a monarch has his people to take care of. The men and women over whom he rules are in the place of his children to him; and he can seldom spare time to love his own children as other parents do. Your father will never be able to leave his kingdom for the sake of seeing his little boy."

This atmosphere of genteel liberal views colors Hawthorne's telling of the story of the rape of Persephone, or Proserpina. He turns her into a dear, sweet girl who could have been asked to tea in Concord by Mr. Emerson or in Cambridge by Mr. Lowell without the faintest risk of anything untoward being done or said. When the first mad days of the elopement are over, Hawthorne's pretty child comes home to wheedle Mumsie out of her huff:

"He certainly did very wrong to carry me off; but then, as he says, it was but a dismal sort of life for him, to live in that great gloomy place, all alone; and it has made a wonderful change in his spirits to have a little girl to run upstairs and down. There is some comfort in making him so happy."

The process of Victorianization is almost complete and
the ground is prepared for rubbish of the kind Goldsworthy
Lowes Dickinson put forward, in 1896, in *The Greek View
of Life:*

> With the Greek civilization beauty perished from the world.
> Never again has it been possible for man to believe that har-
> mony is in fact the truth of all existence.

This belief in harmony, which, according to Lowes
Dickinson, made ancient Greece "that fairest and happiest
halting-place in the secular march of man," sprang like a
flower from the beauty of Greek religion, in which

> all that is unintelligible in the world, all that is alien to man,
> has been drawn, as it were, from its dark retreat, clothed in
> radiant form, and presented to the mind as a glorified image
> of itself.

Alas, the game was up; even while Lowes Dickinson was
writing his fanciful essay, the Greek vision was being dis-
mantled. The host of unmannerly believers in scientific
method who had infiltrated the universities and centers of
polite learning in mid-century, importing with them new
studies such as paleography, linguistics, archeology, and
comparative anthropology, had soon begun to ask all kinds
of coarse and unfeeling questions about the beauties of the
Greek religion. Why, for instance, does Hawthorne's dear,
sweet girl have a Latin name (Proserpina) that means "the
fearful one" and a Greek name (Persephone) that means
"the bringer of destruction"? Any attempt to answer such
questions reduces all the classic myths to a mosaic of unrelated and irreconcilable fragments. While this work of
disintegration was being carried forward, the horns of

feminism were faintly blowing in the outer world, and the
great nineteenth-century revolt against the subjection of
women was getting under way. The picture of a primitive
Greece began to emerge as the liberation of the sex proceeded. By what may well be the purest of coincidences,
Greece had, it seemed, been in early times a matriarchy
in which property had descended not through male heirs
but from mother to daughter. The early altars had been
sacred not to men or to manlike gods such as Zeus and
Apollo but to the triple Goddess of sky, sea, and air, the
Great Mother. Persephone, the bringer of destruction, was,
it appeared, one of her aspects, that spiderlike and far from
winning one in which she castrated her husband with a flint
knife in the furrow of a newly plowed field in order to
secure its fertility and her own. This Greece of the eman-
cipation is a savage society indeed, and it is its mythology
that Mr. Robert Graves reconstructs in his two volumes.
The lyric beauty and the contradictions of the classic myths
are gone. In their place are realism and lucidity applied to
making sense of accounts—scrambled in centuries of religious change—of rituals of sacred marriage, initiation, and
brutal blood sacrifice, in the endless variations on the theme
of the relationship between the Great Mother and the
mortal year king, and to untangling garbled tribal histories
told in a forgotten symbolic language. In each chapter Mr.
Graves puts together his findings on a particular subject,
then appends his bibliography, and follows that with his
own comment. It is perhaps permissible to quote an entire
chapter of the new mythology to show the authority, wit,
and insight he brings to the task of ushering us into the
hag-ridden recesses of the antique mind:

The filthy demons called Empusae, children of Hecate, are ass-haunched and wear brazen slippers—unless, as some declare, each has one ass's leg and one brazen leg. Their habit is to frighten travellers, but they may be routed by insulting words, at the sound of which they flee shieking. Empusae disguise themselves in the forms of bitches, cows, or beautiful maidens and, in the latter shape, will lie with men by night, or at the time of midday sleep, sucking their vital forces till they die.[1]

I. Aristophanes: *Frogs* 288ff.; *Parliament of Women* 1056 and 1094; *Papyri Magici Graeci* iv. 2334; Philostratus: *Life of Apollonius of Tyana* iv. 25; Suidas *sub* Empusae.

1. The Empusae ("forcers-in") are greedily seductive female demons, a concept probably brought to Greece from Palestine, where they went by the name of Lilim ("children of Lilith") and were thought to be ass-haunched, the ass symbolising lechery and cruelty. Lilith ("scritch-owl") was a Canaanite Hecate, and the Jews made amulets to protect themselves against her as late as the Middle Ages. Hecate, the real ruler of Tartarus (see 31. *f*), wore a brazen sandal—the golden sandal was Aphrodite's—and her daughters, the Empusae, followed this example. They could change themselves into beautiful maidens or cows, as well as bitches, because the Bitch Hecate, being a member of the Moon-triad, was the same goddess as Aphrodite, or cow-eyed Hera.

It is to be seen that we have come a long way from the radiant forms of Lowes Dickinson's fantasia and that we are back, after four hundred years, with Cartari's triple-headed and monstrous images. It is hard not to share Burton's feeling that this fountain of ancient fiction has gone brackish, if it ever was sweet, and to avoid his conclusion that mythology should be classified as a disease of the imagination. One feels that this publication marks the end of a chapter in Western cultural history. Mr. Graves has completed, perhaps unintentionally, the work that Sir James Frazer and the scholars of his generation began, of dismantling the vision of a golden age and a lost Eden. We can now see more clearly than ever the Greek intellectual achievement in a reasonable perspective, as the triumph of the rational element in a society schizoid like any other, and warring within itself against the degradation and obscurantism generated by dark and neurotic superstitions.

VILLANOVA COLLEGE LIBRARY

VILLANOVA COLLEGE
LIBRARY